Handing On the Baton

Handing On the Baton

The Conductor as Musicianship Mentor

ALETA KING

WIPF & STOCK · Eugene, Oregon

HANDING ON THE BATON
The Conductor as Musicianship Mentor

Wipf & Stock
An Imprint of Wipf and Stock Publishers
199 W. 8th Ave., Suite 3
Eugene, OR 97401

www.wipfandstock.com

PAPERBACK ISBN: 979-8-3852-6192-5
HARDCOVER ISBN: 979-8-3852-6193-2
EBOOK ISBN: 979-8-3852-6194-9

02/12/26

"The musical education of the child should begin nine months before the birth of the mother."
Zoltán Kodály[1]

To my mother, Barbara King. You gave me the best possible start to my musical education by singing to me from well before my birth.

To my grandmother, Doris Carruthers, who played and sang to my mother before her birth and gave me my first piano lesson at age four.

To my father, Brian King. You drove me to countless music lessons and performances. Whenever I said, "I can't," you said, "You can't *yet*."

And to my grandfather Lawrence Carruthers, who gave me improvisation lessons on the Wurlitzer and multiple other organs and pianos in his basement, which were enough to lure me away from Queensland beaches during summer holidays.

1. Szabó, *Music Education*, 4.

Contents

Acknowledgments

A SINCERE THANK-YOU TO my doctoral supervisors, Associate Professors Jennifer Rowley (thesis) and Neil McEwan (conducting) for your example of expert mentoring.

Thanks and love to my all-time favorite roadie, lyricist, and comedian who sings Handel bass solos in the shower—my irreplaceable husband, Dr. Grenville Kent.

Thanks also to friends and colleagues who cheered me along the way.

Preface

THIS STUDY INVESTIGATES THE conductor's role as musicianship mentor through the rehearsal and performance process of three works for choir and orchestra. The concept of mentoring is examined through three research stages that parallel the three recitals.

In the first stage, twelve participants rehearsing and performing Bach's Cantata BWV 182 were asked about their experience of being mentored by the conductor. Questionnaire and focus group data showed that the conductor's musicianship mentoring role was significant to their progress. They found five musicianship elements most important: inner hearing, musical memory, sight-singing, intervals, and solfège. Of these, solfège was perceived as foundational to developing the other four.

In the second stage, the conductor's self-mentoring process was analyzed using a three-part self-reflective journal during preparation for a performance of Fauré's *Requiem*. Parts A and C explored the core relational aspect of mentoring, while part B reflected on the conductor's self-mentoring process.

In the third stage, four of the original twelve participants were asked about their self-mentoring process during the rehearsal and performance of Karl Jenkins's *The Armed Man: Mass for Peace*. Participants reported that they had acquired the skills to enable self-mentoring and become early-career mentors over two years between the first and third recitals. Inner hearing, sight-singing, intervals, and solfège were again highlighted, as well as ensemble singing and conducting. Participants felt solfège and sight-singing would be most beneficial in the future.

The conductor as musicianship mentor model demonstrates the importance of self-mentoring to mentors and mentees, particularly mentees emerging as mentors. When a pedagogically sequential voice-based musicianship program is intentionally aligned with an ensemble performance program, the resulting synergy has a unique, purposeful, and powerful impact on the teaching and learning environment.

1

Introduction

If you can walk, you can dance,
If you can talk, you can sing.

Zimbabwean Proverb

1.1 I AM HOLDING GUIDO'S HAND IN MY HANDS

I CAN HARDLY BELIEVE I am holding in my two hands a small original fifteenth-century manuscript of Guido's hand from Mantua in northern Italy. I am at Oxford University, and my anticipation is heightened as a small box containing the rare manuscript is brought out of the archives and presented to me in the special collections reading room of the Bodleian Library. I open the box and carefully remove the treasured manuscript from within. Suddenly my senses transport me back in time through six hundred years of history as I savor the first smell of the manuscript, almost a damp, sweet scent like that of an old wine cellar. The manuscript appears old and worn, akin to a much-loved possession. I run my hands over the leather cover, which feels smooth and soft to touch.

The folio pages within are faded and stained yellow with age, and the turning of these brittle pages creates a crisp but faint rustling sound. The black-and-red ink is still remarkably vibrant on the page. The calligraphy is stunning in its neatness and precision, undoubtedly the elegant strokes of a masterful hand. Each page is a treasure chest of lyrics accompanied by early music notation that evokes the spiritual songs of long-forgotten people and their places, objects, beliefs, and ideas.

In the very back pages of this manuscript is the hidden treasure I seek. Before me is one of the oldest surviving examples of the Guidonian hand perfectly preserved. Solmization syllables and early music notation spread across its entire surface area like an intricately detailed aural guide map. As I read the musical symbols, they simultaneously translate into faint but distinct sounds in my head. I quietly reflect on the remarkable fact that this ancient pedagogical tool, first implemented by Guido d'Arezzo almost one thousand years ago (ca. AD 991/992–1033), is one of the oldest existing examples of a pedagogical language that has continued to evolve and is still currently used in twenty-first-century music education.

It occurs to me that Guido's hand means nothing at all without a specialist musician who is both conductor and musicianship mentor to interpret its symbolism, and through the act of singing to bring it to life. In this sense, Guido's hand is about conducting, musicianship, mentoring, and singing, and therefore symbolic of the key elements that comprise the quintessence of this study.

1.2 "IF YOU REALLY WANT TO KNOW MORE, THEN YOU OUGHT TO GO TO HUNGARY"

I was blessed to have inspiring teaching in musicianship during my time as an undergraduate music student in Queensland, Australia. My first-year foundational and second-year intermediate studies introduced me to the concept of musicianship as a discrete skill to be developed in a musician. I had two university mentors who had studied at the Liszt Academy's Kodály Institute in Hungary.

They were both very inspiring teachers who, noticing my obvious enthusiasm for musicianship, encouraged me to go to Hungary for further specialized study. I constantly peppered them with questions, and I vividly recall the day one of them was carrying a heavy box of conducting materials down the stairs of the Music Department. I asked him one question too many as he tried to keep his balance, and he said in a patiently exasperated tone, "Well, Aleta, if you really want to know more, then you ought to go to Hungary." And so I did! (After asking him many more questions about how to get there.) This conversation was the humble beginning that led me to pursue two invaluable years of postgraduate studies in musicianship pedagogy and conducting at the Liszt Academy's Kodály Institute.

During my progression from undergraduate to postgraduate music student, I became increasingly aware that my musicianship and conducting skills had slowly but surely undergone a remarkable transformation during many years of intense study in Australia and Hungary. Most significantly, the secure musicianship foundations laid during my formative years in Australia and strengthened in Hungary continue to remain the fundamental basis upon which my expertise, experience, confidence, and commitment to lifelong learning are built as a professional musicianship mentor and conductor. Unsurprisingly, I wish to inspire the same enthusiasm for excellence in my musicianship and conducting students—hence the reason for my curiosity into my role as a conductor and musicianship mentor. In the same way that my mentors have inspired me, I want to know and understand what my mentees value about the musicianship and conducting legacy passed down from me as their mentor.

1.3 RATIONALE

This thesis is about the conductor whose students use musicianship skills developed in musicianship class through the rehearsal and performance process. The focus of this study is on the correlation between (1) participant experience while completing part or all the musicianship program, (2) their perceived value of the elements of this program when taking part in rehearsals and performances, and (3) the independent application of these skills beyond the program.

There are three purposes to this research study: to examine the role of the conductor as musicianship mentor (CMM) to their mentees; to explore the conductor as musicianship self-mentor; and to investigate how mentees use musicianship skills in their self-mentoring. This research aims to highlight for the conductor the need for self-reflective best practice as a musicianship mentor.

1.4 RESEARCH QUESTIONS

This research was carried out with my students, who were willing participants, and myself as both musicianship mentor and conductor during the rehearsal and performance process of three contrasting works for choir and orchestra. These three recitals were in partial fulfilment of my doctor of musical arts requirements at the Sydney Conservatorium of Music. The mentoring role was examined from three different perspectives through three parallel research questions. Each research question explored the role of the CMM. Below is a summary of the three recitals with their respective research questions:

1. Recital 1, Research Stage 1—Conductor as Mentor to Mentees
   J. S. Bach, Cantata BWV 182, *Himmelskönig, sei willkommen*

   Research Question 1: What is the role of the mentor to mentees in the preparation of a small vocal ensemble (n=12) through the rehearsal and performance process? (questionnaire and focus group discussion)

2. Recital 2, Research Stage 2—Conductor as Self-Mentor
   G. Fauré, *Requiem*

   Research Question 2: What is the conductor's personal self-mentor preparation through the rehearsal and performance process? (reflective journal)

3. Recital 3, Research Stage 3—Conductor's Mentees Become Self-Mentors
   K. Jenkins, *The Armed Man: Mass for Peace*

   Research Question 3: Which musicianship skills have former mentees retained and used in their personal self-mentoring preparation through the rehearsal and performance process, as observed in selected members of the vocal ensemble (n=4) from recital 1? (follow-up interview)

1.5 RESEARCH OVERVIEW

These three public recitals took place across two years. For the first recital (June 2016) I conducted Avondale Conservatorium's twelve-voice chamber choir and eight-piece chamber orchestra in a performance of J. S. Bach's Cantata BWV 182 *Himmelskönig sei willkommen* (Heaven's king, welcome). There were twelve participants in this research, eleven from the choir and one from the orchestra. Of these twelve, nine participants were in my musicianship classes at the Avondale Conservatorium, where selected movements of the Bach cantata were studied concurrently during the rehearsal period. The three remaining participants had been in my advanced musicianship classes within the last three years. At the end of the rehearsal process, each of the twelve participants completed a questionnaire concerning which musicianship skills they had acquired that were most relevant to the cantata. Immediately after the performance, all twelve participants took part in a focus group discussion in which they reflected on which particular musicianship skills the performance had required of them.

For the second recital (October 2016), I conducted the Sydney Conservatorium Symphony Orchestra, Choir, and Chamber Choir in a performance of Gabriel Fauré's *Requiem*. My focus was on the musicianship skills I used in my preparation as a conductor. For this purpose, I kept a self-reflective journal throughout the rehearsal and performance process.

For the third recital (June 2018), I conducted the Newcastle Wind Orchestra and Avondale Singers in a performance of Karl Jenkins's *The Armed Man: Mass for Peace*. This performance included seven of the original twelve participants from the first recital (June 2016). Under my guidance, they had completed the foundational, intermediate, and advanced musicianship levels of their undergraduate musicianship program. As they were no longer students in my class, they were expected to prepare in their own time using the musicianship skills they had acquired and were now teaching to others. Four participants completed a follow-up interview. Two were then working as early career teachers, and the other two were in their final year of music education placements. The follow-up interview asked them to reflect on this change from being a mentee to being able to self-mentor and be a mentor of students.

1.6 THESIS OVERVIEW

This thesis falls into five parts, including this introduction. Chapter 2 will review the relevant literature on musicianship and explore the historical significance of three prominent musicians from the Western art music tradition: Guido d'Arezzo, Johann Sebastian Bach, and Nadia Boulanger. They were selected as preeminent examples of musicians whose mentoring in musicianship was integral to their life as a professional conductor. This chapter concludes with a brief overview of the role of mentoring and its present significance. Chapter 3 outlines the methodology involved in the remainder of this study. Chapters 4, 5, and 6 present the results for each of the three stages of research and discuss their implications. Chapter 7 concludes the study and considers further possible research.

2

Literature Review

Let's start at the very beginning,
A very good place to start.
When you read, you begin with A-B-C,
When you sing, you begin with *do-re-mi.*

MARIA, "DO-RE-MI,"
BY OSCAR HAMMERSTEIN II

2.1 "BUT WHEN IS SHE GOING TO SING?"

IN 2008 I ARRIVED in Honiara, Solomon Islands, with my 1888 German violin in tow. The instrument immediately raised its protest against the humid tropical climate, with its aged wood expanding and sweating and its steel-wound gut strings stubbornly refusing to stay in tune. I stood valiantly to play my solo in the face of mutiny from the tired old instrument. It was clear that most of the audience did not recognize the instrument or know what sound to expect. They looked and listened; some faces expressed curiosity while others showed blank bewilderment before, during, and after my solo. When I sat down, there was polite applause, and one elderly woman whispered not very quietly: "But when is she going to sing?" In this cultural context, it appeared that music and singing were almost synonymous.

Similarly, I often sense just how much singing is at the center of musicianship that permeates everything I do, both as a teacher of musicianship and as a performer on the conducting podium. The synergy between musicianship and conducting, and the role of singing in this process, fascinates me. What is it? Furthermore, why, how, where, when, and with whom does it happen?

This review of the literature begins by defining conducting and musicianship and traces through history the idea of singing as a foundational element to the practice of conducting and musicianship. It highlights the significant contributions of Kodály, Boethius, and Luther. It examines three exceptional musicians, Guido d'Arezzo, Johann Sebastian Bach, and Nadia Boulanger, whose musicianship underpinned their pedagogy and practice as a conductor. It concludes with a brief overview of mentoring in the context of this research study.

2.2 DEFINING CONDUCTING

The origins of conducting as a modern art form can be traced back to ancient Assyrian, Babylonian, Egyptian, and Jewish communal worship practices in which hand gestures were used to lead chanting or singing of hymns, prayers, and sacred texts.[1] During Greek and Roman times, this practice was referred to as *cheironomy*, from the Greek *cheiros*, meaning hand.[2] The history of conducting "may conveniently be divided into three overlapping phases: the singer-timebeater (15th–16th century); the instrumentalist-leader (17th–18th century); the baton conductor (19th–20th century)."[3] These three overlapping phases correspond with the three exceptional musicians at the heart of this literature review: Guido d'Arezzo

1. Feuchtwanger-Sarig, "Chanting to the Hand," 11; Tavierne, "Conducting"; Southerland, "Giving Music a Hand."

2. Gerson-Kiwi, "Cheironomy."

3. Spitzer et al., "Conducting."

provides one of the earliest examples of the singer-timebeater in the eleventh century. Johann Sebastian Bach was a formidable example of the instrumentalist-leader during the first half of the eighteenth century. Nadia Boulanger was an iconic example of the first female baton conductor in the twentieth century.

2.3 DEFINING MUSICIANSHIP

Musicianship has been defined as "the level of musical skill evident in a musician," which recognizes the near truism that the quality of a musician is evidenced by the quality of their musical skills or, in other words, their level of musicianship.[4] This study will assume that excellent musicianship is the foundation of an excellent conductor. The word "musicianship" was added to the *Oxford English Dictionary* only in 1867, yet this does not mean that the concept was unknown historically. There is certainly evidence to suggest that as far back as the classical Greek philosophers, music skill development was integral to music education.[5]

In common with numerous authors (Serafine, McAdams and Bigand, Levitin, Best, Karpinski),[6] this chapter will use the term *musicianship* as a contemporary umbrella term for the wide variety of musical skills that enable a musician's ability to think intelligently in sound.[7] These skills can be variously described in broad terms such as solfège (which is synonymous with the terms tonic solfa, moveable *do*, and/or relative solfa in which *do* is the major tonic and *la* is the minor tonic), music literacy, aural skills, inner hearing, audiating (*audiation* is Edwin Gordon's term for "a cognitive process by which the brain gives meaning to musical sounds,"

4. *Oxford English Dictionary Online*, s.v. "Musicianship."

5. Alperson, "Music Education," 614.

6. Serafine, *Music as Cognition*, 69; McAdams and Bigand, *Thinking in Sound*; Levitin, *Your Brain on Music*; Best, "Music Curricula in Future," 4; Karpinski, *Aural Skills Acquisition*, 4.

7. Serafine, *Music as Cognition*, 69.

"the foundation of musicianship"),[8] auralizing,[9] and ear training. It also encompasses composite fields such as sight-reading, sight-singing, memorizing, listening, dictating, transcribing, arranging, composing, performing, conducting, and directing, though these terms can overlap somewhat in different cultural contexts. There exists a fascinating body of literature on how musicianship is treated in contemporary educational pedagogy, but that is outside the scope of this thesis.

2.4 THE IMPORTANCE OF SINGING IN MUSICIANSHIP

> Musicianship is about training the student not just to be a player of an instrument, but to be a musician.
> The best way to do that is to take the instrument away.
>
> Michael Kaulkin, "What Is Musicianship?"

Hungarian philosopher Zoltán Kodály argued that musicianship in instrumentalists was as effectively developed through singing as for vocalists. After observing the renowned Italian conductor Arturo Toscanini using singing to communicate with his orchestra, Kodály later remarked:

> I heard the finest singing in the world by the world's worst voice—Toscanini's, when at rehearsal he demonstrated a phrase in his blunt, hoarse voice for his players and singers. And this is why they could sing so beautifully under his baton. His most frequent comment to the orchestra was "Cantare! Cantare!" [Sing! Sing!][10]

In teaching this way, Kodály was drawing on a tradition that stretched at least as far back as the Greek foundations of Western

8. Gordon Institute for Music Learning, "Audiation," paras. 2, 1. See also Gordon, *Measures of Music Audiation.*

9. See Karpinski, *Aural Skills Acquisition*, 49.

10. Kodály, "Good Musician?," 193.

civilization.[11] During Kodály's lifetime, his beloved Hungary had endured the forced influence of other cultures, the Austro-Hungarian Empire from 1867 to 1918, later the Nazis until 1945, and finally Soviet Russia. Precisely because of this political turmoil, Kodály advocated for the Hungarian people to rediscover their unique past, identity, and culture through music. Kodály "believed that music should have an essential cultural function and significant social status" in Hungarian society.[12]

Kodály scholar Mihály Ittzés stated: "Kodály's ideas are rooted in various sources which he integrated into his own thinking—a combination that produced his own special philosophy on music education." According to Ittzés, Kodály's philosophy can be summarized as follows: "(i) Music education should be provided in school for all children; (ii) the basis for music education should be singing; (iii) singing is most effectively taught by a value-centered selection of materials based on the music of the mother-tongue (folk music); and (iv) reading and writing of music should be based on relative solmization (moveable doh)."[13]

For inspiration, Kodály turned to Italy and France, drawn by their long tradition of developing musicianship skills centered on singing. Kodály observed: "Music-teaching in Latin countries starts with singing and therefore their instrumental playing also has the nature of singing."[14] This notion resonated with Germany's most prominent nineteenth-century musicians, including Wagner, Bülow, Thalberg, and Schumann.[15] The latter also explicitly encouraged singing in instrumental musical training, demonstrating an awareness of the flaws in the Germanic teaching culture of the time.[16] Heedless of political ideology, Kodály's closing speech to mark the Liszt Academy of Music's 1953 academic year posed the question "Who is a good musician?" and concluded that the

11. Plato, *Republic*, 93.
12. Ittzés, "Zoltán Kodály," 132.
13. Ittzés, "Zoltán Kodály," 132.
14. Kodály, "Good Musician?," 193.
15. Kodály, "Good Musician?," 192–93.
16. Schumann, *Advice to Young Musicians.*

required characteristics were a well-trained ear, a well-trained intelligence, a well-trained heart, and a well-trained hand. He wrote:

> All four must develop together, in constant equilibrium. As soon as one lags behind or rushes ahead, there is something wrong. So far, most of you have met only the requirement of the fourth point: the training of your fingers has left the rest far behind. You would have achieved the same results more quickly and easily, however, if your training in the other three had kept pace.[17]

Kodály referred to this "general training in musical skills" development as "technique généralé."[18] To aid this general technical training in music skill development, Kodály gathered the best music education practices of the time: from Italy, Guido d'Arezzo's solmization and music literacy; from France, Pierre Galin, Aimé Paris, and Émile Chevé, who contributed rhythm names;[19] and from England, Sarah Glover, who pioneered tonic solfa, and later John Curwen, who developed hand signs to compliment the solfa syllables.[20] Much later, this would come to be known by others outside of Hungary as the Kodály philosophy or method. Kodály, his students, and successors openly acknowledged his borrowing, as the focus was not so much on creating a so-called "method" but rather about utilizing whatever best resources were available to create a quality music education culture. This eclecticism helped to create a formidable music education system embedded in Hungarian cultural practices, with singing at its core.

Kodály is not without his critics. Bennet Reimer is best known for his leading contributions to aesthetic music education philosophy in the 1970s and 1980s. He is, therefore, quite critical of music education methodologies he believes to be narrowly aligned to practical performance rather than aesthetic music education ideals in which the musical work exists as an autonomous object to be

17. Kodály, "Good Musician?," 197.
18. Ittzés, "Zoltán Kodály," 133.
19. Rainbow, "French Time Names."
20. Rainbow and McGuire, "Tonic Sol-Fa."

studied independently of any performance of the work.[21] Reimer refers to the Kodály concept as "active musicianship, construed primarily as the ability to perform."[22] In this regard, Reimer's aesthetic music education ideals appear to be far from Kodály's beliefs about what constitutes quality music education. During the 1990s, Reimer's former doctoral student David Elliott developed what he called a praxial philosophy of music education,[23] "in which the act of making music (*musicing*) reminds us that performing and improvising through singing and playing instruments lies at the heart of music as a diverse human practice."[24] Elliott is opposed to the aesthetic music education philosophy in which the musical work, not the performance of the work, is most important.[25] Complementing this, Howard Gardner defines music as a unique way of knowing and doing in his theory of multiple intelligences.[26] Elliott's and Gardner's ideas together emphasize the practical experience (over the aesthetic experience) inherent in music's unique way of knowing and doing, which more closely aligns with the Kodály concept of music education.

Outside of Hungary, the work of Kodály continues to make a significant impact in research scholarship and best practice in musicianship skill development programs in the higher music education context. Recent examples of scholarly teaching and learning resources that are specifically aimed at the practical application of Kodály's concepts in higher music education musicianship programs include Micheál Houlahan and Philip Tacka's *From Sound to Symbol: Fundamentals of Music* and the current work of Mónika Benedek and David Vinden in *Harmony Through Relative Solfa*. Kodály's contribution is also acknowledged within a broader scholarship context. Two significant examples of these include

21. Reimer, *Philosophy of Music Education* (1989), 150–67.

22. Reimer, *Philosophy of Music Education* (2003), 245.

23. For concise definitions, see Elliott and Silverman, *Music Matters*, 17; Elliott, *Praxial Music Education*.

24. Elliott, *Music Matters*, 49.

25. Elliott, *Music Matters*, 29–38.

26. See Gardner, *Frames of Mind*; *Multiple Intelligences*.

contributions from Ida Vujović[27] and Gary Karpinski, whose seminal work on the acquisition of aural skills in higher music education refers to the Kodály concept and places emphasis on using a tonic-centric solmization system for skill development.[28] With this contemporary foundation established, it is pertinent to examine historical traditions that have held to variations of the concept.

2.5 MUSIC EDUCATION IN CLASSICAL ANTIQUITY

Music was one of the seven liberal arts of Greek classical education, and philosophers, including Plato, Aristotle, and Pythagoras, viewed it as essential to the development of society.[29] Pythagoras understood the physical world as a "material working out (representation) of numerical truth, and that this truth is immediately and easily apprehended, albeit superficially, in elementary musical consonances."[30]

The first level of a liberal arts education was the *trivium* (an intersection of three roads), which included the study of the art of words and language acquired through grammar (input), logic (process), and rhetoric (output). The second level of liberal arts was referred to as the *quadrivium* (four roads), which included a study of the art of numbers or mathematics, acquired through arithmetic (pure numbers), geometry (numbers in space), music (numbers in time), and astronomy (numbers in space and time). These seven liberal arts laid the foundation for the third level, which was considered the pinnacle of Greek education: the pursuit of truth and morality through philosophy and theology.[31] The Greek liberal arts scholar pursued this quest for truth by acquiring and mastering the art of thinking. However, as Plato scholar

27. Vujović, "Between Building Foundational Skills."
28. Karpinski, *Aural Skills Acquisition*.
29. Beck and Thomas, "Greek Education," 489.
30. Barbera, "Pythagoras."
31. Joseph, *Trivium*, 3.

Desmond Lee observes, "Greek music was employed largely as an accompaniment to song."[32] Music, then, made rich connections between the spoken word of the trivium and the numbers in time of the quadrivium and was considered essential to intellectual development. It elevated the spoken word into singing, with or without instrumental accompaniment.

While Greek music education valued the pursuit of truth through the development of moral character and intellect, Roman culture seemed more interested in the practicalities of life. Barker provocatively suggests the Romans reacted to Greek philosophies regarding music because the "Romans seem to have thought of the musical elements in education either as a source of peripheral gentlemanly adornments or as a part of a thoroughly ungentlemanly professional training." In the Roman era, music seemed to lose the elite philosophical status it had enjoyed in Greece, taking a more practical role to meet the functional demands of sacred and secular rituals in Roman society. Poetry breaking away from music was a significant reason for this change of status. As Barker notes, "Sophisticated poetry had emancipated itself from occasions of musical performance and was primarily designed to be spoken or read."[33]

At the same time, musical instruments gradually moved beyond the mere accompaniment of vocal performance to become solo instruments in their own right, thereby eroding the central role that singing had once enjoyed in secular music performance. This progression predictably influenced music education, giving rise to separate and distinct instrumental performance practices that relied less on the Greek philosophical emphasis on music's ability to influence the development of moral character in favor of a more Roman practical emphasis on the technical and theoretical study of music.[34]

32. Lee, in Plato, *Republic*, 93.

33. Barker, "Music," 975.

34. Barker, "Music," 975.

2.6 BOETHIUS

The "primary figure in the transition between the intellectual worlds of Classical Antiquity and the Middle Ages" was the Roman philosopher Anicius Manlius Severinus Boethius (AD 477–524).[35] In his treatise *De Institutione Musica* or *Fundamentals of Music*, Boethius compares the four mathematical arts of the quadrivium and singles out music as significantly different from the other three. He argues that music possesses the unrivalled potential to appeal to both intellectual reason and the physical senses. Further, it can therefore provide logical truth as well as evoke a pleasurable physical sound sensation, or even an offensive one.[36] Boethius suggests that music has the power to connect the intellectual with the physical, which is a desired outcome of integrated musicianship education to this day. Boethius confers the title *musicus* (musician) on the one who was considered musical, that is, skilled in the theoretical and philosophical understanding of music first and foremost.[37] As a Platonist whose philosophy valued the soul more highly than the body, Boethius tended to privilege the theoretical and philosophical over the practical skills.

Boethius recognized three kinds of music.[38] *Musica universalis* (also called *musica mundana*) meant the sound residing in the universe as envisaged in Pythagoras's theory of the harmony of the spheres.[39] *Musica humana* referred to the sound of the right relations between soul and body. He regarded these first two kinds of music as being inaudible to the bodily senses; the music of the spheres was too loud for the ears to hear but could be sensed by the soul. The music constituted in certain instruments, *musica quae in quibusdam constituta est instrumentis*, included the voice as an instrument. For Boethius, "The voice, operated with the air and with

35. McKinnon, "Boethius."

36. Boethius, "Fundamentals of Music," 2:138.

37. Boethius, "Fundamentals of Music," 2:142.

38. Boethius, "Fundamentals of Music," 2:140.

39. Proust, "Harmony of the Spheres"; Gaizauskas, "Harmony of the Spheres."

the tongue as plectrum, was, of course, as much an instrument as any artificial musical instrument."[40]

2.7 EARLY CHRISTIAN ERA

As Christianity increasingly permeated the Roman culture, vocal performance again returned to prominence. Early Christian church music was almost exclusively vocal, having developed out of Jewish and Byzantine chant traditions.[41] Five significant early Christian church fathers, Basil, John Chrysostom, Jerome, Niceta of Remesiana, and Augustine, all expounded upon the virtues of singing and the chanting of biblical psalms.[42] The liturgical chant had become the central focus of music in the early Christian church. So music education at this time centered on the practical development of the voice for chanting and singing in worship.

Rome had inherited Boethius's ideas about what constitutes a true musician (*musicus*). However, this ideology, in which the theoretical and philosophical was more important than performance ability, was increasingly challenged by the practical realities of Christian worship that demanded regular performances and lacked time to develop a theoretically and philosophically well-trained *musicus*. Pesce suggests the *musicus* ideal was no longer plausible and that since "the church needed performers of chant . . . performance could no longer be relegated to a second seat."[43]

2.8 GUIDO D'AREZZO

From this eleventh-century musical backdrop, Guido d'Arezzo emerged to become one of the earliest conductors and musicianship mentors in Western art music history. Originally known as

40. Burnett, "Sound in Middle Ages," 71.

41. Conomos, "Early Christian and Byzantine."

42. Basil, "Homily on First Psalm"; John Chrysostom, "Exposition of Psalm 41"; Jerome, "Commentary on Ephesians"; Niceta of Remesiana, "Benefit of Psalmody"; Augustine, "Confessions."

43. Pesce, "Guido d'Arezzo," 25–26.

Guido Monaco (Guido the monk), he was educated at Pomposa Monastery, where he quickly established himself as a notable singing teacher and vocal ensemble director. As McKinnon observes, "Guido's reputation reached mythic proportions, but there is no denying that he was a musical theorist of singular intelligence and originality."[44] Guido's originality of thought can be attributed partly to his rejection of overly philosophical Greek ideas in favor of a more practical approach to meet the professional demands of his life as a musician. Guido boldly asserted that he was "not following Boethius, whose treatise is useful to philosophers but not to singers."[45] Pesce suggests that "Guido had little use for the speculative inquiries of the *musicus*, for he needed to train boys to sing chant as efficiently as possible. As a result, understanding had to serve the act of singing."[46] Guido faced fierce criticism from his contemporaries in the universities, who insisted the art of music be primarily studied theoretically and philosophically as part of the traditional quadrivium of classical antiquity. As such, they saw little use in learning the practical application of Guido's pedagogical methods.[47] In this sense, Guido was well ahead of his time when compared to his academic contemporaries.

Nevertheless, Guido did not want his singers merely to memorize by rote learning. His understanding of the term "musician" is best clarified by the distinction he makes between the musician and the singer. In his treatise *Regule Rithmice*, Guido laments the divide between musicians and singers, stating that "the latter talk about what music comprises, while the former understands these things. For he who does what he does not understand is termed a beast."[48] These were harsh words aimed at singers serving in the context of sacred medieval worship. Guido needed to transform his singers into musicians in which both theoretical understanding and practical performance facility were intrinsically linked.

44. McKinnon, "Guido of Arezzo."

45. Guido d'Arrezo, "Prologue to His Antiphoner," 2:218.

46. Pesce, "Guido d'Arezzo," 26.

47. Hornby, "On Guido's Handiwork," 123.

48. Pesce, *Guido d'Arezzo's "Regule Rithmice,"* 330–33.

Pesce states that Guido "clearly derided a singer who remained the 'unknowing' cantor and wanted a singer to be independent of a teacher and, ultimately, to be able to sight-sing a melody."[49]

Prior to Guido's innovations, educating musicians had traditionally relied on oral dissemination via rote learning, repetition, and memory to perpetuate music aurally from teacher to student. Guido considered this approach unnecessarily laborious, time consuming, often unreliable, and even "childish."[50] Guido, the experienced pedagogue, identified the inefficiencies of always having to rely on rote learning from the external sound of an instrument or another voice to learn one's part. Years of practical experience meant he understood the inevitable shortcomings of this approach, which prompted the following observation: "I have seen many keen-witted philosophers, not only in Italy, but also in France and Germany, and even in Greece, try this approach but not become what I would call musicians, or even singers, unable to match the ability of our choirboys."[51]

To promote musical understanding in his singers, Guido focused on developing the *sensus*, which he defined as the mind and body. In his prologue, Guido states that "in every art, exceedingly more numerous are the things that we learn through our *sensus* than those that we have learned from a teacher."[52] This concept of *sensus* echoes the philosophical thoughts of Boethius. It can be defined in two ways: corporeal and mental, with corporeal being defined as the body's physical perception, feeling, or sensation of something, and mental being defined as the mind's intellectual reason or moral understanding of something.[53] For Guido, therefore, musical understanding was what intrinsically happened at the nexus between the body and the mind, where the physical senses and the mental intellect intersect. Guido's absolute commitment to

49. Pesce, "Guido d'Arezzo," 26.

50. Guido d'Arezzo, "Epistle Concerning Unknown Chant," 2:216.

51. Guido d'Arezzo, "Epistle Concerning Unknown Chant," 2:216.

52. Guido d'Arezzo, "Prologue to His Antiphoner," 2:211.

53. Pesce, "Guido d'Arezzo," 26.

musical understanding as a pedagogical outcome is why he is one of three historical figures central to this thesis.

Guido's epistle outlines the pedagogical method he developed to impart musical understanding to his singers.[54] First, a brief explanation of the hexachord is necessary to understand the context of Guido's pedagogical method. The hexachord was named for its grouping of a six-pitch tone set or scale. The three basic hexachords F-G-A-Bb-C-D; C-D-E-F-G-A; G-A-B-C-D-E had already been well established in Greek music theory. According to scholars, "The hexachords beginning on C, G, and F received the names 'natural', 'hard' and 'soft' (*naturale, durum, molle*) respectively."[55] The primary interval sequence inherent in a hexachord tone set is, therefore, tone-tone-semitone-tone-tone. Guido's genius was in creating a method to assist with memorizing or internalizing the property or function of each pitch in relation to every other pitch within any given hexachord tone set. Pesce observes that "in directing his singers to internalize the *proprietas* or property of every pitch by means of this vehicle, Guido called into play both sensory perception and intellect."[56]

In his epistle, Guido first mentions the use of the plainchant hymn "Ut Queant Laxis" in relation to his method. The chant text appears to have existed from about the ninth century, though scholars generally acknowledge the composer of this chant melody to be unknown. Significantly though, the melody is arranged so that each successive phrase begins one note higher. This would suggest inherent pedagogical purposes embedded into the construction of the melody that very likely attributes its melodic compositional origins to Guido.[57]

Analysis of the first verse of "Ut Queant Laxis" reveals four interesting features. First, it is written on the F clef in Roman chant notation,[58] and therefore the start pitch of the opening phrase is

54. Guido d'Arezzo, "Epistle Concerning Unknown Chant," 2:217–18.

55. Hughes and Gerson-Kiwi, "Solmization."

56. Pesce, "Guido d'Arezzo," 25.

57. See Guido d'Arezzo, "Epistle Concerning Unknown Chant," 2:217.

58. Referred to as the "fah clef" in Benedictines of Solesmes, *Liber Usualis*,

the C that corresponds to the lowest pitch of the C hexachord (C-D-E-F-G-A). Second, the first verse is divided up into seven short phrases. When comparing the first six phrases of this melody, each successive phrase starts on the next ascending pitch of the C hexachord. Third, five of the seven phrases conclude on D, the apparent tonal center of this melody and suggesting the D Dorian mode. This also explains why the seventh phrase adds contrast and balance to the melodic shape through an organic descending melodic line that comes to a close on the D tonal center. Finally, if the first syllable of each of the first six phrases is isolated, the following syllabic pattern results: *ut, re, mi, fa, sol, la.*

These syllables *ut, re, mi, fa, sol, la* are the prototype for what became known as the solmization system to aid aural recognition still in use in the Western world today. Guido developed his solmization system as a practical way to achieve the desired result: giving his singers the ability to read music. Allaire clarifies this point further by suggesting that "solmisation was to both the medieval and the renaissance musician what solfeggio or solfège is to the modern: a means to an end—more specifically, a technique for the development of accuracy in reading and singing music."[59] *Ut* eventually gave way to *do*, and the seventh pitch *si* was later added as the hexachord extended to the eight-note diatonic scale.

Guido's first important innovation was to develop the solmization syllables that were primarily an aural mnemonic aid for singers. Guido's second innovation was to develop a visual mnemonic aid to complement them: he assigned the solmization syllables of the hexachord to specific parts of his hand. Known affectionately as Guido's hand (see fig. 3), this diagram served as an intermediate step between solmization syllables and staff notation.

xvii.

59. Allaire, *Hexachords, Solmisation*, 43.

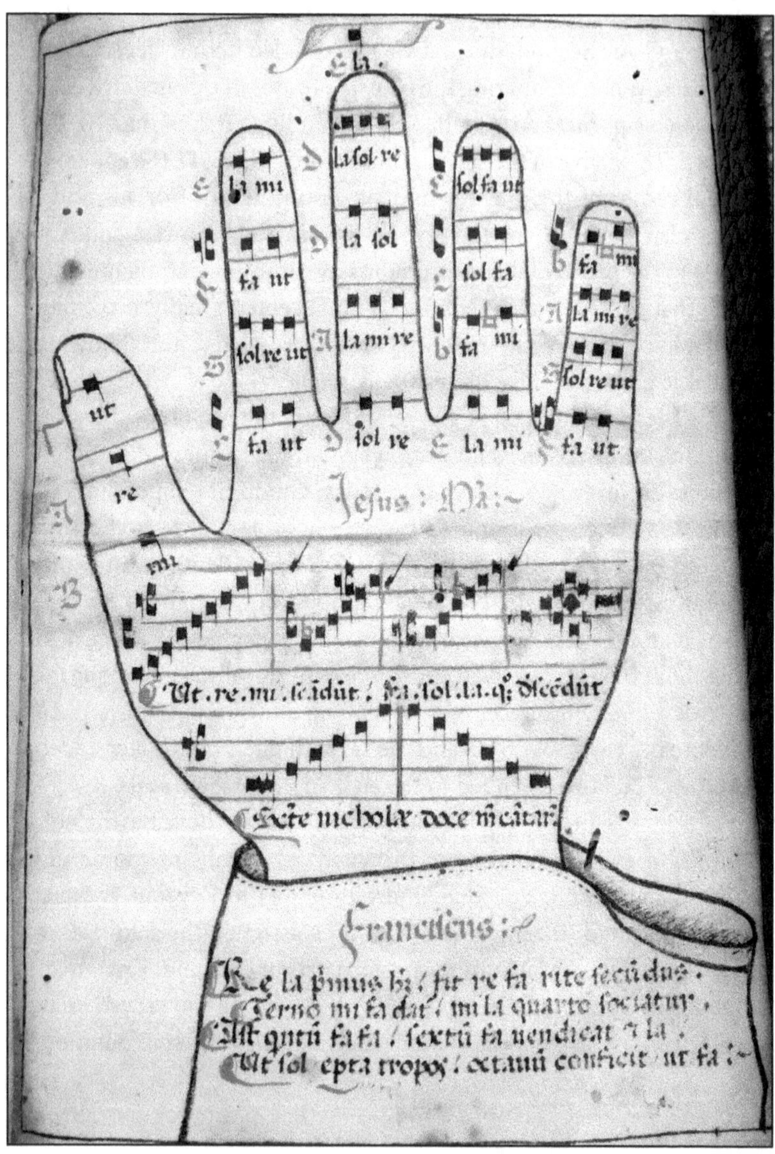

Figure 1: Guido's Hand. Photographed by the author.[60]

60. Guido d'Arezzo, "Guidonian Hand."

Following these developments, Guido's third innovation was to connect these intermediary steps with early staff notation. There appears to be a scholarly consensus that early notation (neumes), pitch names, and the practice of solmization were already in existence in some form well before Guido.[61] However, Guido's genius was to draw all these elements together to develop a unique pedagogical system of music literacy that combined solmization syllables, hand signs, and a more cohesively standardized staff notation to give precise pitch and facilitate accurate, instantaneous sight-singing of previously unknown music.[62] Because of these innovations, Guido's work has significantly impacted music literacy across every century since and continues to do so today. The particular importance of solmization's influence can be summarized as follows:

> It has been mistakenly supposed that solmisation had become obsolete and redundant even before the 16th century or, at best, that it was used solely by beginners who, having once acquired a good technique of music reading, had no further need for its principles and rules. We do not support the view that musicians invariably learned their music with the aid of solmisation syllables. What we do believe is that, after having acquired adequate reading facility, the musician could indeed sing or play without reference to these syllables, *but in accordance with the rules of the system*, just as a modern musician performs at sight without recourse to solfeggio. In short, solmisation was to the medieval and renaissance musician what spelling is to the reader. Once sufficient ability has been developed, reading becomes a simple automatic process.[63]

It is important to note, however, that this significant pedagogical shift towards musical literacy did not mean that the eyes (visual) were considered superior to the ears (aural) or that the ear was no longer required or was somehow subservient to the eye.

61. Haines, "Origins of Musical Staff," 328.

62. Hornby, "On Guido's Handiwork," 123.

63. Allaire, *Hexachords, Solmisation*, 43–44.

On the contrary, it was by formalizing a system of solmization, and using the Guidonian hand as an intermediary pedagogical step of visual representation connected to aural perception that led eventually to the reading of staff notation. Thus, Guido effectively refined and strengthened the organic connection between the eyes (sight) and ears (sound) as equal partners in the musical literacy process. Thinking intelligently in sound requires both aural and visual analytical skills to work together and inform one another. This process is quality music literacy in action.

Guido's most profound contribution was undoubtedly facilitating the fundamental shift towards music literacy. His primary motivation for advancing the cause of music literacy would seem a matter of practical efficiency. However, Guido also appears to have been imbued with a sense of divine purpose. He refers to his new pedagogical approach as a "favour divinely bestowed upon me . . . so that those who come after . . . learn with the greatest ease the ecclesiastical melodies which I and all my predecessors learned only with the greatest difficulty."[64] He also saw the results as near miraculous:

> We do not need to have constant recourse to the voice of a singer or to the sound of some instrument to become acquainted with an unknown melody so that as if blind, we should seem never to go forward without a leader; we need to implant deeply in memory the different qualities of the individual sounds and of all their descents and ascents. You will then have an altogether easy and thoroughly tested method of finding an unknown melody, provided there is someone present to teach the pupil, not merely from a written textbook, but rather by our practice of informal discussion. After I began teaching this procedure to boys, some of them were able before the third day to sing an unknown melody with ease, which by other methods would not have been possible in many weeks.[65]

64. Guido d'Arezzo, "Epistle Concerning Unknown Chant," 2:215.
65. Guido d'Arezzo, "Epistle Concerning Unknown Chant," 2:217.

Guido had developed and refined a music literacy system whereby he was able to speed up this transfer between theoretical musical knowledge and practical musical understanding. Guido's innovations in musical education were driven by his choristers' need to learn the sheer volume of monastic chants efficiently in order to perform them at a suitably high standard. One small step for Guido became one giant leap for Western art music. His new pedagogical method attracted wide attention, arousing admiration and jealousy among his peers, and even gained him an unexpected private audience with the pope. Guido later decided to move to a monastery just outside the town of Arezzo, which became one of the traditional custodians of his pedagogical innovations, as well as his namesake.

2.9 MARTIN LUTHER AND MUSIC EDUCATION IN THE REFORMATION ERA

Guido's patriarchal contributions to musicianship education were driven by his practical role as a conductor and musicianship mentor. So too was Martin Luther's contribution driven by the pragmatic needs of music education during the time of the Protestant Reformation in Germany. Martin Luther is best known for his prominent role in initiating the Reformation, but he was also an accomplished composer and musician, the product of a traditional Latin education. As Guido before him, Luther's educational experience and his future ideals grew out of Greek and Roman music education traditions embodied in German Latin schools of the time. A typical Latin school (equivalent to an English grammar school) in the heartland of Luther's pre-Reformation and post-Reformation Germany was arguably a variation on the ancient Greek educational ideals in which the study of music through the science of singing was an integral part of the trivium and quadrivium.[66]

Luther "affirmed music as a gift of God and argued for the inclusion of good music in education for its influence on moral

66. See Gardiner, *Bach*, 39.

development," particularly in young people.[67] In the foreword to his hymnbook, Luther insists that the young "should and must be trained in music and in other proper arts" to enable them to "yield willingly, as becomes them, to the good."[68]

There are several reasons why music education played a crucial role in Luther's Reformation. During the Middle Ages and Renaissance, singing was an integral and universal part of cultural life throughout Europe. Singing was the way to learn and transmit information in a largely illiterate oral culture, and people expected to listen and learn in this way. For Luther, all music was spiritual and helpful for the development of one's theological worldview. As such, Luther composed new music and borrowed from artistic models and sacred melodies, using lyrics to impart sacred truths orally. One of his central values was that religion was for the people, not just the clergy, and that every person should be able to read the Scriptures (assisted by Gutenberg's recent invention of the printing press), think for themselves, and worship in their native language. Singing, then, was vital to education and worship.[69]

For this reason, singing remained a central component of music education, particularly in Germany's Latin schools of Martin Luther's era. It appears that the headmasters of these German Latin schools doubled as the cantor: the singing teacher, choir director, and music educator. In this context, it is unsurprising that Luther remarked, "A schoolmaster must be able to sing; otherwise, I won't acknowledge him."[70] For Luther, like Guido before him, singing was the focus point of quality music education.

2.10 JOHANN SEBASTIAN BACH

In keeping with Lutheran tradition, Johann Sebastian Bach was educated at a Latin school in his birth town of Eisenach, deep in

67. McCarthy and Goble, "Music Education, Philosophy of."
68. Luther, "Wittenberg Gesangbuch," 3:362.
69. Doukhan, *In Tune with God*, 161–99.
70. Gardiner, *Bach*, 39.

the heart of Reformation territory. Although Bach's musical family environment likely laid the foundations for his earliest informal musical education, Gardiner suggests that "ultimately the responsibility for a child's [formal] musical education lay with the local cantor." According to German traditions of the time, the cantor could also have been the schoolmaster, the director of church (sacred) music, the director of town (secular) music, or a combination of two or all three. The young Bach's enrolment at the Eisenach Latin school between the ages of eight and ten probably meant that he auditioned for the town's local church choir at Georgenkirche at the suggestion of the school cantor. The audition requirements for this choir indicate an expected understanding of "clefs, time signatures and rests" and an ability to "sing at sight a fugue, motet, and concerto."[71] This would suggest that these musicianship skills were necessarily developed specifically through the medium of singing.

When Bach arrived in Lüneberg at the age of fifteen to join the elite St. Michael's Cloister chamber choir on a scholarship, effectively indicating he was a "poor singing scholar,"[72] he was expected to be able to "sing fluently in canon and to be able to read at sight polyphonic motets of the Renaissance as well as the more complex music by recent and modern composers."[73] Bach would later expect the same rigorous musicianship of his pupils, with training that also included "mastery of thoroughbass and voice-leading in four-part chorales before attempting inventions of their own"[74] and an ability to "work out their musical ideas mentally."[75] In other words, they were expected to develop a mastery of inner hearing or audiation. When asked to give a reason for his astonishing musical prowess as an adult, he is said to have replied, "I was obliged to work hard; whoever is equally industrious will succeed just as well."[76] Similarly, when complimented on his impressive

71. Gardiner, *Bach*, 66.

72. Geck, *Johann Sebastian Bach*, 42.

73. Gardiner, *Bach*, 66.

74. Gardiner, *Bach*, 209.

75. Forkel, *Johann Sebastian Bach*, 96.

76. Forkel, *Johann Sebastian Bach*, 106. See also Gardiner, *Bach*, 209.

organ skills, Bach responded dismissively: "There is nothing very wonderful about it; you have only to hit the right notes at the right moment, and the instrument does the rest."[77]

A thirty-eight-year-old Bach was likely very experienced in matters of musicianship training upon arrival in Leipzig to take up his new appointment as cantor of St. Thomas School and music director for the city.[78] Bach's formative years of training in the musical traditions of Latin schools had undoubtedly equipped him for his new appointment as cantor at St. Thomas School. Here he was expected to mentor his students in rigorous musicianship skill development with singing at the core, which constituted the music education of his time. It was in Bach's best interests to ensure that his St. Thomas schoolboys received a quality music education, and therefore, the musicianship mentoring tradition continued.

Bach's son Carl Philipp Emanuel, writing in his father's obituary, listed the musicianship skills that made the elder Bach such a fine composer: "Harmonising, realizing figured bass, transposing, handling clefs, transcribing, studying and copying scores, composing by inventing ideas, mastery of harmony enough to create full-voiced music."[79] None of this would have been possible without Bach's foundational music experience as a chorister in the Latin school traditions. Comparing German musical education ideals with those of Italian and English choir schools of the time reveals many shared values. Italian choir boys "received intensive daily training in the singing of chant, polyphony, counterpoint, and new music";[80] English choir boys in the elite Chapel Royal Choir received daily singing lessons and music theory.[81] Evidently, singing was assumed to be at the core of quality musicianship education, which was, in turn, the mark of a quality musician.

Perhaps the most revealing of Bach's thoughts on his role as musicianship mentor can be found in the pages of his personal

77. Spitta, *Johann Sebastian Bach*, 3:262.

78. Geck, *Johann Sebastian Bach*, 115.

79. Williams, *Bach*, 2016.

80. Heller, *Music in the Baroque*, 149.

81. Heller, *Music in the Baroque*, 151.

study Bible.[82] Of particular interest is the Old Testament book of First Chronicles, in which King David selects 288 musicians: "All of them trained and skilful in music . . . for the ministry of prophesying, accompanied by harps, lyres, and cymbals" (1 Chron 25:1). They were all "under the direction" of various leaders; usually their fathers, all of whom in turn worked "under the order of the king" (25:6), a clear structure of mentoring that combined "the small as well as the great, the teacher with the student" (25:8). Bach's handwritten note in the right-hand column at the beginning of this chapter (see fig. 4) enthuses: "NB. Dieses Capitel ist das wahre Fundament aller gottgefälliger Kirchen Music usw" (Note: This chapter is the true foundation of all God-pleasing church music, etc.).[83] This Bible contained Luther's translation and commentary and additional commentary by Abraham Calov and was part of Bach's extensive personal theological library. Bach's "Lutheran faith is of the utmost significance for [his] creative work,"[84] judged by the fact that "a high proportion of Bach's music, unlike that of his peers, was addressed to a church congregation, rather than a lay audience. Religion was central not just to his upbringing and his education but to the locus of his employment and his general outlook on life."[85] Clearly then, this biblical chapter was a part of Bach's very personal commitment to mentoring, which he took very seriously as his sacred calling.

Boethius, Guido, Luther, and Bach all inherited the legacy of generations who had gone before them. They each had a significant influence on the music education of their time and helped to create a legacy for future generations of music educators. Approximately 150 years after Bach, we observe Zoltán Kodály, another who had a remarkable influence on the music education of his time. Kodály looked back to these influential historical figures, as well as to his

82. See facsimile in Leaver, *Bach and Scripture*, 93–94.

83. See Cox, *Calov Bible*, 418. A literary analysis of this text can be found on p. 22.

84. Geck, *Johann Sebastian Bach*, 653.

85. Gardiner, *Bach*, 125–26.

peers, to clarify what he understood as the way forward for music education in the early twentieth century.

2.11 NADIA BOULANGER

Nadia Boulanger was a contemporary of Kodály, who similarly had a distinctive influence on music education in the last century. Boulanger provides an inspiring and outstanding example of the CMM model. Boasting an impressive musical pedigree, she excelled in solfège, harmony, fugue, organ, piano accompaniment, and composition while a student at the elite Paris Conservatoire, where she was also a finalist (1907) and second-prize winner (1908) in the prestigious Prix de Rome competition for young composers. However, it was not primarily as a composer that Boulanger was to make her mark on the musical world. She was candid with interviewer Bruno Monsaingeon: "I realized at twenty that I wasn't a composer. That was so obvious! The music I have written is what I call useless!"[86] Nadia believed that her beloved sister Lili Boulanger possessed greater talent as a composer, but Lili tragically died at the age of just twenty-four while Nadia's career spanned seventy-five years and included the roles of teacher, conductor, organist, and even composer.

Although she is perhaps best remembered as an outstandingly gifted teacher, she was also one of the first professional female conductors. As Jeanice Brooks asserts, "Her astonishing success was due to a combination of factors, chief among them her undeniable musicianship and legendary charisma. But Boulanger's achievement was also due to her successful negotiation within a culture unwilling to accept female conductors."[87] It was Boulanger who conducted the international premiere performance of the *Requiem* by her beloved composition teacher Gabriel Fauré in London in 1936. In both capacities as pedagogue and conductor,

86. Monsaingeon, *Nadia Boulanger*, 51:11. See also Campbell, *Master Teacher*, 31.

87. Brooks, "Noble et grande servant," 92.

she was nationally and internationally recognized in her lifetime and remains iconic to this day.

Boulanger has been described as "the most influential teacher since Socrates,"[88] and her students form an illustrious list of over 250 leading composers, arrangers, and conductors, including Daniel Barenboim, Lennox Berkeley, Idil Biret, Elliot Carter, Aaron Copland, David Diamond, John Eliot Gardiner, Philip Glass, Roy Harris, Quincy Jones, Gilbert Levine, Dinu Lapatti, Igor Markevitch, Julia Perry, and Laurence Rosenthal.[89] Nevertheless, she did not refer to herself as a teacher of composition; rather, she called herself a teacher of technique.

What exactly was Boulanger's technique? She forcefully told Monsaingeon, "A draconian technique!"[90] He then asked her to describe what happens first when a new student comes to consult with her. She responded, "I make him work at solfeggio with Mademoiselle Dieudonné." Dieudonné had been Boulanger's pupil for fourteen years and became one of her closest confidantes. Some pupils appreciated her thoroughness, while "others remarked that she completely lacked Boulanger's gifts of communication."[91]

Evidently, Boulanger's "technique" can be understood to mean musicianship, which will be discussed below. Boulanger's teaching method is known only through her students, as she never published any teaching materials, and "she was always keen to emphasise that the musical work, rather than the performer or a commentator on the music, should be the center of attention."[92] It is evident then that the "great composers" of the Western art music tradition and "the masterpieces they wrote" were foundational to her teaching methods.[93] Her students' accounts consistently reveal a pattern of rigorous musicianship skill development, leading to thorough and fluent training in what she believed to be the

88. Rorem, Review of *Nadia Boulanger*.

89. www.nadiaboulanger.org.

90. Monsaingeon, *Nadia Boulanger*, 36:07.

91. Potter, *Nadia and Lili Boulanger*, 130.

92. Potter, *Nadia and Lili Boulanger*, 130.

93. Potter, *Nadia and Lili Boulanger*, 128.

primary technical foundation required of every serious professional musician. These foundational elements included solfège,[94] clef reading, score reading, transposition, figured bass realization, harmony, counterpoint, and score analysis.[95]

Boulanger's students came first from Paris and, as her fame gradually spread, eventually from across Europe and America. Composers Aaron Copland and Virgil Thompson were two of the first American students to study with Boulanger in the early 1920s. From that time onwards, a steady stream of American music students undertook the pilgrimage to Paris. In his autobiography, Philip Glass recalls Virgil Thompson's famous remark, "Every town in America has a drugstore and a student of Boulanger."[96] Boulanger referred to her American pupils as "brilliant students, very talented people, but the grounding isn't secure in many cases, their ear isn't developed: the basics haven't been drummed into them."[97] American choral conductor Harriet Simons, after her first conducting lesson with Boulanger, stated, "I was very angry at all former teachers and professors for somehow failing to teach me as much as I needed to know in order to prepare me for life as a professional musician. My education in music had finally begun!"[98] Simons said further:

> I had gone to France to study conducting, but I soon discovered that all of us, regardless of intended focus of study, spent most of our time in classes of harmony and solfège. We also participated in choral rehearsals that summer of Bach's Cantata 4 and Fauré's *Requiem*, works we also studied in conducting class. I thought, of course,

94. The use of solfège in the French music educational context means that *do* equals C, and therefore this fixed-pitch system of reading notation is often referred to as *fixed do*. This is in direct contrast to Guido d'Arezzo's original intention that *ut* (which later became *do*) was simply the first note of "Ut Queant Laxis," in which *re* was the tonal center.

95. Potter refers to some of these elements as auxiliary disciplines (*Nadia and Lili Boulanger*, 128).

96. Glass, *Words Without Music*, 129.

97. Monsaingeon and Boulanger, *Mademoiselle*, 29–30.

98. Simons, "Nadia and Me," 324.

> that my days of studying music theory were long behind me . . . [but] we were expected to sing, play harmonic progressions, conduct and do music every day. All elements seemed to be considered equally important.[99]

Lennox Berkeley, a noted English composer and one of Boulanger's first European students from the 1920s, rhapsodized about the value of her technique to his development as a composer:

> Nadia Boulanger teaches that the composer must first be a good workman who knows his job, and that then only is he free to write what he likes, and to realize whatever ideas he has: that it does not matter how much drudgery you go through to gain that freedom, for a man must lose his life in order to find it, and in music he must lose his originality and personality in order to find them. Moreover, there is no risk in the case of a man who has really got something to say that he will become dry and pedantic through a severe technical training.[100]

For Berkeley, Boulanger was more than just a teacher of technique. "She [was] a teacher of the art of music as a whole . . . she infused into her pupils that power of self-criticism and discipline which is so essential to the composer."[101]

Philip Glass, the eminent American composer, spent two years during the mid-1960s studying with Boulanger in Paris. In his autobiography, Glass gives an intriguing insight into his time with her. He studied the entire first book of Bach's preludes and fugues in the first year, followed by all of Mozart's piano concertos in the second. His harmony studies began with first species counterpoint, Renaissance music, sight-reading, solfège, figured bass, clef reading (all seven C clefs!), transposition into all keys, the regular weekly task of learning a four-part Bach chorale in open score using original C clefs, then singing and playing cadences and chord progressions in every key, and improvising soprano, alto, tenor, or bass parts over a given melodic line in the style of Bach,

99. Simons, "Nadia and Me," 325.

100. Berkeley, "Letters to Nadia Boulanger," 49.

101. Berkeley, "Letters to Nadia Boulanger," 48.

following all the usual rules of voice leading. Glass summarized his learning experience as follows:

> Slowly, over those two years, her teaching began to take root in me, and I began to notice a marked difference in the way I could "hear" music. My attention and focus became heightened, and I began to hear music in my "inner" ear with a clarity I had never had until then, even suspected was possible. I became able to have a clear audio image in my head. I could hear it, I knew what it was, and also—something a little bit more difficult than that—in time, I could hear something I hadn't heard before, and I could find a way to write it down. That is actually quite hard to do and a major accomplishment by itself.[102]

Glass goes on to explain the result of Boulanger's development of technique in her students:

> I would describe it this way: If you wanted to be a carpenter, you would learn how to use a hammer and a saw and how to measure. That would be basic. If someone said, "Here, build a table," but you had never done it before, you would pick up the tools and maybe you could build a table, but it would be shaky and probably a mess. What Mlle. Boulanger taught was how to hold a hammer, how to use a saw, how to measure, how to visualize what you were doing, and how to plan the whole process. And when you had learned all that, you could build a really good table. Now, she never thought the "table" was itself music composition. She thought her training was simply about technique. Basically, when you left her, if you had studied with her diligently, you would end up with a toolbox of shiny, bright tools that you knew how to use. And that was a tremendous thing. You could build a table, you could build a chair, you could put in a window—you could do anything that was needed.[103]

102. Glass, *Words Without Music*, 133–34.

103. Glass, *Words Without Music*, 129–30.

Like Berkeley, Glass also maintained that Boulanger taught much more than mere technique.[104] He describes technique as the key to understanding a composer's overarching signature style or unique fingerprint. He recalls the day near the end of his two-year study with Boulanger when he realized that he had transitioned from learning technique to talking about style:

> I had thought she was teaching technique—the how you "do" or "not do" in music. But that was over. She had raised the ante. Now we were talking about style. In other words, there could be many correct solutions to a musical problem. Those many correct solutions came under the rubric of technique. However, the particular way a composer solved the problem . . . became the audible style of the composer. Almost like a fingerprint . . . style is a special case of technique . . . that in a nutshell is what Mademoiselle Boulanger was teaching.[105]

In 1974, her seventieth year of teaching, Boulanger was interviewed by the prominent Hungarian musician and author Bálint András Varga. Boulanger recounted her musical education in her formative years:

> We were lucky in that we received a thorough elementary technical education early on: solfeggio, sight-reading, ear-training—all of which is beyond the reach of so many children nowadays. We only acquire it at twenty-five or twenty-eight when it is too late: we ought to have begun at five. After all, it would be absurd if we only started to learn reading at twenty-five. If one has a lively imagination but has not got the necessary background, one can end up in a dangerous situation. I may be wrong; in any case I do believe that *if we do not know a language, we cannot express ourselves in it.*[106]

Boulanger's convictions about developing technique, as shown in her teaching style, are similar to Kodály's views on the

104. Glass, *Words Without Music*, 133.

105. Glass, *Words Without Music*, 134–35.

106. Varga, "Nadia Boulanger," 191; emphasis added.

importance of rigorous and systematic musicianship education from a very early age in order to become fluent in the language of music. Kodály's protégé Erzšébet Szönyi was his conduit to Boulanger. He arranged for Szönyi to learn from Boulanger, and when she returned to Hungary, she adapted the teaching techniques she had learned.[107]

Quite clearly, Boulanger's technique was built upon a solid pedagogical foundation of musicianship skill development with singing at the core, a foundation that she considered central to the success of every professional musician, especially conductors. Notably, two of the most lauded conductor-composers of the twentieth century, the Russian Igor Markevitch and the Jewish American Leonard Bernstein, repeatedly credit Nadia Boulanger's influence on their careers.[108] And significantly, the foundation Boulanger espoused is essentially the same as those of the figures examined in this literature review so far: Greek philosophers, Boethius, Guido d'Arezzo, Martin Luther, Johann Sebastian Bach, and Kodály.

2.12 MENTORING

The concept of mentoring and the related concepts of self-mentoring and peer-mentoring are central to this thesis. Mentoring, self-mentoring, and peer-mentoring through the literature will be explored here to give greater contextual meaning to the CMM model explained in more detail in the methodology chapter of this thesis.

Historically, the popular belief among scholars is that the concept of mentoring can be traced back to ca. 750 BC with the ancient Greek classic *Odyssey.* Odysseus leaves his young son Telemachus in the care of a trusted friend and guardian called Mentor.[109] There is strong circumstantial evidence to suggest that the mentoring concept existed as far back as ca. 5000 BC in ancient

107. Jaccard, *Tear in the Curtain*, 51–66.

108. Monsaingeon, *Nadia Boulanger.*

109. Irby et al., "Epistemological Beginnings of Mentoring," 19.

Egypt.[110] As Clutterbuck et al. state: "Many cultures, on all inhabited continents, have philosophical traditions that include the role of a wise companion, who joins a younger person on their journey towards maturity and wisdom of their own. Sage, guru, elder—all have similar elements, including the use of metaphor or narrative, and the posing of questions that provoke reflection and insight."[111] A prominent example of this would be King Solomon, who exemplified the Hebrew sapiential tradition and was reputed to have been the wisest man of his time. Much of his sage advice is encapsulated in the Old Testament wisdom books of Proverbs, Ecclesiastes, and Song of Songs.[112]

While the current discourse around the concept of mentoring would suggest that there is no single definition, most scholars agree that mentoring is fundamentally about relationships. The earliest and most used definitions center on the relationship between an older or more experienced person (the mentor) and a younger or less experienced person (the mentee). As Kerka expands, "Mentoring is typically defined as a relationship between an experienced and a less experienced person in which the mentor provides guidance, advice, support, and feedback to the protégé."[113] Other definitions allow for a breadth and depth of understanding that would suggest "mentoring is, in its most basic form, a developmental relationship grounded in and [molded] by philosophical, historical, and sociological factors . . . there is also a basic tendency to personify mentoring as a relationship between an older, more experienced mentor and a younger, less experienced mentee."[114]

Mentoring in relation to this thesis is situated within the higher education context, and as such, two interpretations are utilized. The first by Patricia Castanheira aptly applies to the context of higher education: "Mentoring as a developmental relationship in which the mentor shares knowledge and expertise to support

110. Irby et al., "Epistemological Beginnings of Mentoring," 20–26.

111. Clutterbuck et al., introduction to *SAGE Handbook of Mentoring*, 3.

112. Alter, *Wisdom Books*, xiii–xiv.

113. Kerka, "New Perspectives on Mentoring," 1–2.

114. Dominguez and Kochan, "Defining Mentoring," 3.

the mentee's learning and professional development."[115] Perhaps more importantly, the second interpretation outlines that the mentor relationship has the capacity for transformation, elegantly described by Bean et al.:

> Mentoring is first and foremost a relationship. The mentor can be all or one of the following: a trusted [counsellor], coach, tutor, advisor, trusted guide, trainer, advocate, and/or role model. At its best, mentoring can be a life-altering relationship that inspires mutual growth, learning, and development. Its effects can be remarkable, profound, and enduring; mentoring relationships have the capacity to transform individuals, groups, organizations, and communities.[116]

Mentoring, through the mentor-mentee relationship utilized in this research project, is more akin to what is understood to be the American model of mentoring. This model "involves a one-way learning process where a mentor is a sponsor or advocate for a protégé and is often an experienced individual in the same field."[117] This is particularly relevant to stage 1 (with the author/conductor as mentor and participants as mentees) and stage 3 (where participants become mentors to mentees of their own) of this research topic, outlined further in the methodology chapter 3 and the results and discussion chapters 4 and 6.

Self-mentoring is a variation of the core model of mentoring in which one intuitively mentors their curious self through a gathering of accessible resources that results in a learning process ultimately aimed at a better awareness, an enlightened way of knowing, and a clearer understanding.[118] Self-mentoring strategies may include actively seeking out a mentor; conversing with knowledgeable or skilled others; consulting online or hard-copy information in the form of books, journals, and articles; seeking professional

115. Castanheira, "Mentoring for Educators' Learning," 334.

116. Bean et al., "Mentoring in Higher Education," 57.

117. Lancer et al., *Techniques for Coaching*, 5–6.

118. Garvey et al., "First-Person Mentoring." For a concise overview of self-mentoring in the higher education context, see Carr et al., "Learning to Lead."

development opportunities; or even simply solving challenges independently.[119] These strategies are often innately utilized without a conscious awareness that they are, in fact, forms of self-mentoring.

William T. Holmes and Marsha Carr frame self-mentoring as "self-initiated training practice [with] four-tiered, self-paced and individualised levels . . . that build on skill development from the previous level."[120] These four levels are "self-awareness, self-development, self-reflection, and self-monitoring."[121] Overall, they identify that "as a growth mindset, self-mentoring is both cyclical and forward-thinking regarding expectations."[122] This mentoring model is particularly relevant to research stages 2 and 3 of this research topic as outlined in chapter 3 and further explored in the results and discussion chapters 5 and 6.

Mentoring, through the peer mentor relationship, is a specific type of mentoring that "entails the informal sharing of information or expertise from people of the same or similar rank as well as colleagues across rank."[123] In this regard, peer mentoring is more akin to what some thought leaders refer to as the European model of developmental mentoring in which the mentor helps the mentee "develop their own high-quality thinking. The mentor has wisdom and experience but uses them to help the mentee become courageous and develop their own wisdom rather than to impart knowledge."[124] This mentoring model is particularly relevant to research stage 2 of this research topic outlined in the methodology chapter (3) and the results and discussion chapter 5. The concept of mentoring, in particular mentor-mentee relationships, self-mentoring, and peer-mentoring relationships, permeates the methodology, results, and discussion chapters of this thesis.

119. Darling, "Self-Mentoring Strategies."

120. Holmes and Carr, "Motivating Language and Self-Mentoring," 4–5.

121. Holmes and Carr, "Motivating Language and Self-Mentoring," 5.

122. Holmes and Carr, "Motivating Language and Self-Mentoring," 5.

123. Davis et al., "Peer Mentoring and Inclusion," 445.

124. Lancer et al., *Techniques for Coaching*, 5.

2.13 CONCLUSION

This literature review began with a focus on defining musicianship and its importance to the development of the CMM. A brief historical survey of key periods of Western art music history, beginning with Greek foundations and continuing through Roman, early Christian, Reformation, and Baroque eras up to the twentieth century, highlights the importance of musicianship and demonstrates how often singing was placed at the core of musicianship development. Three musicians stand out amid this historical timeline due to their expertise as both conductors and musicianship mentors, namely, Guido d'Arezzo, Johann Sebastian Bach, and Nadia Boulanger. All three demonstrably valued excellent musicianship skills as significant to their personal self-mentoring development and to the development of those they mentored. The following chapters will endeavor to show that the strength of a conductor and the CMM model comes from this strong foundation of musicianship, of which singing is a core component.

3

Methodology

In one short, spicy sentence,
musicianship is what your ear hears
while you are conducting.

ELIZABETH A. H. GREEN, *THE MODERN CONDUCTOR*

3.1 RESEARCH DESIGN

IN EXPLORING THE MUSICIANSHIP-MENTORING role of the conductor, the research design utilized a mixed-methods approach containing elements of both qualitative and quantitative research data interwoven with the accompanying recitals. This particular design had the characteristics of a qualitative method and analysis with a small but significant amount of quantitative data. The research data collection tools employed comprised a questionnaire, focus group discussion, and follow-up interview for recital participants, and a self-reflective journal for the conductor.

The three-recital format of the doctor of musical arts program necessitated three parallel research stages, and data collection was spread across these stages over a period of two years. Each stage highlighted a different aspect of the conductor as musicianship mentor (CMM) role. The research data tools examined the CMM role from three distinct yet complimentary perspectives: conductor as a mentor to mentees; conductor as self-mentor; and conductor's mentees become self-mentors. A triangulation approach was taken to data analysis, allowing the results of each stage to inform and interrogate each other. Cohen, Manion, and Morrison provide the following definition for triangulation in the context of research design:

> The use of two or more methods of data collection in the study of some aspect of human behaviour . . . triangular techniques . . . attempt to map out, or explain more fully, the richness and complexity of human behaviour by studying it from more than one standpoint and, in so doing, by making use of both quantitative and qualitative data. Triangulation is a powerful way of demonstrating concurrent validity, particularly in qualitative research.[1]

Potential participants were identified using purposive or criterion-based sampling: as students and members of my choir.[2] To alleviate any bias and or coercion, all participants were volunteers. The first stage and recital examined the CMM to their mentees. The second stage and recital focused on the conductor as musicianship self-mentor. The third stage and recital considered the conductor's original mentees emerging as their own self-mentors.

3.2 RECITAL 1: J. S. BACH, CANTATA BWV 182, *HIMMELSKÖNIG, SEI WILLKOMMEN*

The first research stage of this study explored the role of the conductor as a musicianship mentor to their mentees during the rehearsal and performance process. The first doctoral recital was a performance of J. S. Bach's Cantata BWV 182, *Himmelskönig, sei willkommen*, on June 3, 2016, in Recital Hall West at the Sydney

1. Cohen et al., *Research Methods in Education*, 195.
2. Burns, *Introduction to Research Methods*, 465.

Conservatorium of Music.[3] With an eye to historically informed performance, I wanted to perform this cantata with a vocal ensemble of twelve voices (three per part) and a chamber orchestra consisting of a mix of period and modern instruments: flute, violin (concertante), violin (ripieno), two violas, cello (continuo), violone (continuo), and harpsichord. The study participants were music students (past and present) from the Avondale Conservatorium who were enrolled in the musicianship program and were also members of the small vocal ensemble Avondale Chamber Singers. Participants were invited to participate in this stage of the research study, and all twelve members of the ensemble agreed. They then completed a pre-performance questionnaire and took part in a post-performance focus group discussion.

3.2.1 Musicianship Program

In my role as director of music at Avondale Conservatorium, I purposefully integrated elements of the Bach Cantata BWV 182 into the repertoire for my musicianship classes during semester 1, 2016. Time spent studying any excerpts in the musicianship program can be considered part of the rehearsal process. These classes covered three levels of musicianship—foundational (first year), intermediate (second year), and advanced (third and fourth year). Musicianship classes at each level were offered for two hours per week over thirteen weeks, giving a total of twenty-six hours per semester. Of the twelve participants, three were recent graduates who had completed all three levels of musicianship and were not currently enrolled in these classes. Of the remaining nine participants, eight had completed the foundational and intermediate levels and were enrolled in the advanced level, and one participant had completed the foundational level and was currently enrolled in the intermediate level.

Musicianship students at all levels were initially introduced to the cantata through the study of the chorale melody "Jesu, deine

3. For a recording of this performance, see https://youtu.be/gGemspiyyxY.

Passion."[4] This melody appears in the key of G major as the foundation of the soprano part of the seventh choral fantasy movement of the cantata. Additional harmonizations of this particular chorale melody can be found among standard J. S. Bach chorale collections. All nine current musicianship students were given the E-flat major chorale harmonization as a sight-singing exercise. Foundational students were asked to make a basic aural and visual analysis of the tonal centers of each phrase. Intermediate students did the same and added a harmonic analysis of the cadence points of each phrase. Advanced students completed a full, detailed, aural and visual analysis of the harmonic progression of each phrase in the chorale. They also completed a detailed harmonic and formal analysis of the chorale melody in the context of the chorale (seventh movement) in the cantata.

Advanced students also studied this chorale harmonization through various technical exercises: singing each of the soprano, alto, and tenor voice parts against the bass line as a two-part sing-and-play exercise on the piano; singing each part against other parts as three- and four-part sing-and-play exercises on the piano; singing one voice per part in SATB quartets; and conducting their peers in a performance of the chorale, utilizing recently acquired foundational conducting techniques. Further, these students also studied the opening sonata movement through formal analysis and harmonic analysis, and performed it by singing the tenor and alto C clef parts while simultaneously accompanying themselves at the keyboard with a simple figured bass line. Advanced musicianship students also studied the bass recitative (third movement) through initially singing the melody while playing the continuo bass line and then by taking turns conducting their peers as bass recitative soloists and continuo players.

4. J. S. Bach's harmonization of Paul Stockmann's 1636 chorale melody appears as no. 194 in E-flat major in Bach, *Chorale-Gesänge*, 129. This particular "Jesu, deine Passion" chorale is a setting of verse 33.

3.2.2 Avondale Chamber Singers

The twelve participants had been invited to sing with the Avondale Chamber Singers for the cantata's three choral movements. Ten of the twelve participants attended weekly sectional and tutti rehearsals over a period of twelve weeks, while the remaining two participants joined rehearsals closer to the performance. For the performance itself, eleven of the twelve participants sang (three sopranos, three altos, three tenors, three basses) with the Avondale Chamber Singers, and one participant joined the chamber ensemble to play violin (ripieno) for the entire cantata.[5] In addition to singing as part of the small vocal ensemble, one other participant briefly joined the orchestra on violin for the instrumental sonata movement. Another took on the role of understudy to the bass soloist, and another was the alto soloist for the performance.

3.3 RESEARCH STAGE 1: CONDUCTOR AS MENTOR TO MENTEES

For this first stage, the research question was defined as: *What is the role of the conductor as musicianship mentor to mentees in the preparation of a small vocal ensemble (n=12) through the rehearsal and performance process?* The data collection tools utilized for this first research stage were the questionnaire and focus group discussion. After human ethics approval, the students identified as potential participants were sent a letter of invitation into the study. This email also included the participant information statement as an additional attachment. Any student who subsequently agreed to take part in this study as a confirmed participant was given a hard copy of the participant consent form and invited to sign it prior to the recital on June 3, and was given the questionnaire to

5. This participant was a principal study violinist. So, although they chose to sing with the chamber choir during rehearsals, they were expected to play in the chamber orchestra for the performance to meet the ensemble performance assessment requirements.

fill out. Immediately after the performance, all participants took part in a guided debriefing in the form of a focus group discussion.

Both the questionnaire and the focus group were designed to elicit each participant's perception about the value of musicianship to the rehearsal and performance stages of this cantata. The focus group facilitation emphasized narrative inquiry, looking for themes and key words to complement the questionnaire and bring to light any further aspects. Participants were also invited to take part in a follow-up interview later. The research data collected from the first stage of this study completed questionnaires, and the transcription of the focus group discussion was first analyzed in June 2016. Together they provided a rich source of information and revealed students' perceptions of how the musicianship classes had affected their preparation through the rehearsal and performance stages of the Bach cantata. This first stage of research formed the basis of a paper presented at the Oxford Conducting Institute's inaugural International Conducting Studies Conference at St Anne's College, Oxford, on June 24, 2016. This paper was also presented at the Kodály Music Education Institute of Australia's biannual national conference in Brisbane on September 29, 2016, and again at the Australian Society for Music Education's twenty-first national conference in Melbourne on July 17, 2017. It was subsequently published in the latter's conference proceedings.[6]

3.3.1 Questionnaire

The pre-performance questionnaire comprised twelve questions grouped into four parts. The first part of the questionnaire (questions 1–8) involved the collection of demographic information that helped to define the background profile of each participant. Demographic information was compiled on a spreadsheet for comparison between participants. The second part (questions 9–10) listed the various elements of musicianship that participants had studied and asked them to rank these elements by their relevance

6. King, "That's a Lot of Dots!"

to the preparation process during the rehearsal and performance stages of the Bach cantata. The collected data were subsequently analyzed quantitatively, as discussed in chapter 4. The questionnaire's third part (question 11) allowed participants to give an open-ended response identifying which elements of musicianship covered in class were most helpful to their preparation through the rehearsal and performance stages of the cantata and to elaborate on why. These responses were also graphically represented on a spreadsheet for comparison and were subsequently analyzed using color coding to highlight key words. These key words were later grouped into emerging themes that will be discussed in chapter 4. The questionnaire's fourth and final part (question 12) asked participants to indicate by way of a yes/no response whether they were willing to be involved in a follow-up interview at a later stage. All participants agreed to this.

3.3.2 Focus Group Discussion

The focus group discussion took the form of a thirty-minute debriefing session immediately after the final performance. This discussion was audio- and video-recorded, and a full transcription was made of the dialogue. This transcript was then analyzed, first for key words and later for emerging themes. These results are discussed further in chapter 4.

3.4 RECITAL 2: GABRIEL FAURÉ, *REQUIEM*

The second research stage of this study occurred in tandem with the second recital and considered the conductor's role as self-mentor during the rehearsal and performance process. The second doctoral recital involved a performance of Gabriel Fauré's *Requiem* with a large chorus of approximately eighty voices and a symphony orchestra. The combined forces of the Sydney Conservatorium Choir, Chamber Choir, and Symphony Orchestra performed the concert, with Associate Professor Neil McEwan as conductor for the first performance on Friday, October 21, and myself as the conductor for the second performance on Saturday, October 22, 2016, in Verbrugghen Hall at the Sydney Conservatorium of Music.[7]

3.5 RESEARCH STAGE 2: CONDUCTOR AS SELF-MENTOR

For this second stage, the research question was defined: *What is the conductor's personal self-mentor preparation through the rehearsal and performance process?* The research data collection tool utilized for this second research stage was a self-reflective journal divided into three parts. Part A logged my self-reflective thoughts on the time spent working with the choir, part B journaled my self-preparation process as a conductor, and part C logged my self-reflective thoughts on the time spent working with the orchestra.

3.5.1 Self-Reflective Journal

In order to address the research question, I kept a self-reflective journal and regularly made observational field notes that focused on three main areas. First, it summarized key learnings in my role as assistant conductor to Associate Professor Neil McEwan, the then director of the Sydney Conservatorium choral program and conductor of the conservatorium choir and chamber choir. Second, it noted insights gained from my role as guest conductor for Dr. Eduardo Diazmuñoz, who was artistic and musical director and chief conductor of the conservatorium symphony orchestra at the time. Finally, it detailed how musicianship influenced my preparation as a conductor during the rehearsal and performance process. This part of the self-reflective journal outlines the technical and musical aspects of my preparation. Articulating these aspects also developed my own researcher's voice to describe the dual roles of conductor and musicianship mentor from my

7. For a recording of this performance, see https://youtu.be/FaeIZ7RKnnc (StageCam); https://youtu.be/DKEREBeUGWQ (HouseCam)

subjective viewpoint. Perhaps not surprisingly, many of the musicianship skills I expected of myself were the same as I expected of my participants. The journal concludes with a consideration of the emerging relationship between my conducting mentors and myself. The dissemination of this journal is the focus of chapter 5.

3.6 RECITAL 3: KARL JENKINS, *THE ARMED MAN: MASS FOR PEACE*

The third research stage of this study aligned with the third and final recital and examined the conductor's mentees, who had since become self-mentors during the rehearsal and performance process. The third doctoral recital was a performance of Karl Jenkins's *The Armed Man: Mass for Peace* on June 2, 2018, at Avondale University Church.[8] Of the original twelve participants from the first recital, seven took part in the small vocal ensemble for this final recital performance.

This recital performance also happened to be the Australian premiere of Martin Ellerby's arrangement, scored for soloists, chorus, and symphonic wind orchestra. In April 2000, Karl Jenkins premiered his original scoring of *The Armed Man: Mass for Peace*, conducting the London Philharmonic Orchestra and the National Youth Choir of Great Britain. In 2010 Ellerby arranged the work for symphonic wind orchestra. My colleague Dr. Ian Cook, director of Newcastle Wind Orchestra, was aware of the existence of this new wind orchestra arrangement along with the fact that it had not yet been performed in Australia. He suggested a collaboration between the Newcastle Youth Orchestra and Avondale Conservatorium choirs in an Australian premiere performance.

This creative vision eventually grew to include collaborations with an additional choir, dancers, and a narrator. Kathryn Dries was invited to be the alto soloist. The invitation was extended to her community choir, Port Harmony Inc., to further augment the choral forces by combining with Avondale Singers. Working with

8. For a recording of this performance, see https://youtu.be/muE1U-RM-Dvg (StageCam); https://youtu.be/xnOka16J5rY (HouseCam).

two separate choral ensembles can bring its own set of unique challenges, and both Kathryn and I were acutely aware of the importance of a consistent blend in choral sound between the two choral entities. As the director of the Avondale choral program, it would be easy for me to facilitate the crafted choral sound I was after.

Additionally, I decided to direct the first rehearsal with Port Harmony to lay the foundation for musical interpretation. Kathryn and I also kept in close contact to exchange music interpretative ideas throughout the choral rehearsal process. When the two choral entities finally came together for the first tutti rehearsals in the week before the scheduled performance, the biggest challenge was blending the two choral entities quickly to achieve a homogenous choral sound.

The majority who sing with the Avondale Choral program are university students between the ages of eighteen and twenty-two, with a few additional Avondale alumni and community members. Due to this age range, there is a natural tendency towards a lighter, breathier, more youthful choral sound with a smaller vibrato. In contrast to this, Port Harmony is a community choir, with most members between fifty and seventy years of age. There is a tendency toward a heavier, less breathy, larger vibrato, more mature choral sound. In the performance context, I realized the importance of standing positions, having learned this during my undergraduate studies under the direction of the late Dr. John Nickson and seen it endorsed in the choral work of James Jordan at Westminster Choir College of Rider University in Princeton, New Jersey, and demonstrated in Weston Noble's film work.[9] The first consideration was to voice-place the small vocal ensemble (which included the seven participants) at the front and center of the choir. Following this, the remaining choristers from Avondale and Port Harmony were voice-placed surrounding the small vocal ensemble.

9. See Noble, *Achieving Choral Blend.*

3.7 RESEARCH STAGE 3: CONDUCTOR'S MENTEES BECOME SELF-MENTORS

For this third stage, the research question was defined as: *Which musicianship skills have former students retained and used in their own personal self-mentoring preparation through the rehearsal and performance process, as observed in selected members of the vocal ensemble (n=4) from recital 1?* The research data tool utilized for this third and final research stage was the follow-up interview.

All of the original twelve participants were invited to take part in the performance; however, only seven participants (two undergraduate pre-service teachers and five graduate teachers) were available for the performance, which took place on June 2, 2018, at Avondale University Church. The participants were all part of the small vocal ensemble at the core of the large choir for the chorus numbers: "The Armed Man" (first movement), "Kyrie" (third movement), "Sanctus" (fifth movement), "Hymn Before Action" (sixth movement), "Charge" (seventh movement), "Agnus Dei" (tenth movement), "Benedictus" (twelfth movement), and "Better Is Peace" (thirteenth movement). Additionally, they performed as part of the small vocal ensemble for "Save Me from Bloody Men" (fourth movement), "Torches" (ninth movement), and the final a cappella "God Shall Wipe Away All Tears" (thirteenth movement). Two of the seven participants were also soloists for the "Kyrie" (third movement), "Angry Flames" (eighth movement), and "Better Is Peace" (thirteenth movement).

3.7.1 Follow-Up Interview

The purpose of the follow-up interview was twofold. First, it examined how participants perceived the impact or benefit of cumulative musicianship skills across the two years between the first and third recitals. Second, it examined how selected participants who had been mentees from the first research stage might have progressed to self-mentors and even the mentorship of others by the third research stage.

The remaining seven participants had agreed in writing two years earlier to participate in the follow-up interview. However, to ensure there was no coercion, each of the seven participants was again invited to take part in the interview voluntarily. All seven participants responded in the affirmative. The week before the final recital, the seven participants were emailed a copy of the follow-up interview questions.

In the week after the recital, a reminder email was sent. Four of the seven participants responded: two undergraduate pre-service music teachers and two graduates who were early-career music teachers. Three participants did not respond even after two additional reminder emails. My research focused on the four remaining participants. No longer actively mentored by me in musicianship and conducting, they were now self-mentoring, and three of the four had experiences of mentoring their students. This follow-up interview was intended to examine how they now viewed the connection between musicianship and performance. In effect, I was asking how effectively the baton had been handed on.[10] I presented findings from this third stage of research at the Oxford Conducting Institute Second International Conducting Studies Conference at St Anne's College, Oxford, on June 22, 2018, and again at the Kodály Music Education Institute of Australia's biannual national conference in Perth, on October 2, 2018.

3.8 CONCLUSION

This study centered its three research stages around the three major recitals. The first used a questionnaire and focus group discussion to collect data on the role of musicianship in the conductor's role as musicianship mentor to student mentees. The second used a self-reflective journal to collect data on the role of musicianship in the conductor's self-mentoring process. The third consisted of a follow-up interview to collect data on the role of musicianship in each of the remaining four participants' transition from mentee to

10. King, "Handing On the Baton."

self-mentor and mentor of others. The results of this three-stage, mixed-methods research study outlined above will be discussed in more detail in the following chapters.

4

Results and Discussion: Recital 1 | Research Stage 1

At the heart of great musicianship
is the ability to manipulate in one's mind
rich representation of the desired soundscape.

Daniel Levitin and Scott Grafton,
"Measuring the Representational Space"

4.1 RECITAL 1: J. S. BACH, CANTATA BWV 182, *HIMMELSKÖNIG, SEI WILLKOMMEN*

This recital comprised a live performance of Johann Sebastian Bach's Cantata BWV 182, *Himmelskönig, sei willkommen*, together with a critical commentary highlighting aspects of historically informed performance practice relevant to this work.

4.2 RESEARCH STAGE 1: CONDUCTOR AS MUSICIANSHIP MENTOR TO MENTEES

The purpose of this first research stage is to focus on the conductor's role as a musicianship mentor to mentees. In this paradigm, I am the conductor and musicianship mentor, and the participants in this research stage are my mentees. The results for this stage were gleaned from the written and verbal responses of the twelve participants through two primary data sources—a questionnaire and a focus group discussion.

Each of the twelve participants was asked to fill out the questionnaire immediately prior to the first recital. All twelve participants took part in a focus group discussion immediately after the first recital. The questionnaire results, together with the transcript of this focus group discussion, form the raw data from which the results were gathered. Therefore, this chapter will consider participant responses to questions 9 and 11 of the questionnaire and the focus group discussion. Finally, these two data sets will be compared and contrasted to highlight any emerging themes, where appropriate.

4.3 QUESTIONNAIRE: QUESTION 9

Question 9 focused on specific musicianship elements integral to musicianship skill development in musicianship classes. Participants (identified as P1–P12) were asked to rate each of the forty-six listed musicianship elements in relation to its perceived degree of relevance to participants through the Bach cantata rehearsal and performance process. The ratings were established on a five-point Likert scale as 5 = extremely relevant, 4 = very relevant, 3 = somewhat relevant, 2 = not relevant, 1 = not applicable.

Nine of the twelve participants (P2, P3, P4, P5, P6, P9, P10, P11, P12) were currently in my musicianship classes. The remaining three participants (P1, P7, P8) had been in my musicianship classes in previous years but were not current students. Their responses to question 9 at times showed they understood this question as not applicable to them. Nevertheless, the data results suggested an apparent consensus among most participants regarding which musicianship elements were considered most important. Of the forty-six musicianship elements listed, thirty-seven received lower overall ratings with an average score of 3.9 or below and were therefore not considered for further analysis. The remaining nine musicianship elements received higher overall ratings with an average score of 4.0 or above and were considered for further analysis. The average for these highest-rated musicianship elements was 4.4, a significant mean score for a five-point Likert scale. These nine elements are listed in descending order in figure 5.

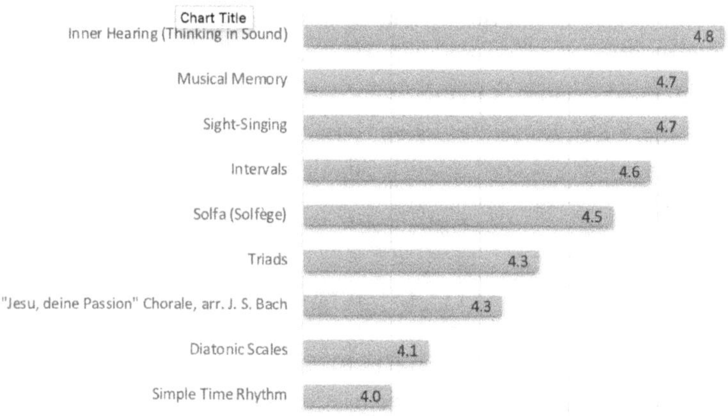

Figure 2: Question 9 Analysis (Highest-Rated Musicianship Elements)

4.4 QUESTIONNAIRE: QUESTION 11

The nine highest-scoring musicianship elements from the twelve participants' responses at question 9 were examined in relation to question 11, which asked for open-ended responses about which musicianship elements the participants viewed as most helpful throughout the rehearsal and performance stages of the Bach cantata.

4.4.1 Inner Hearing

Inner hearing was the consistently highest-ranked musicianship element, considered very relevant (three participants) and extremely relevant (nine participants) to the rehearsal and performance process. Three of the twelve participants (P1, P3, P4) referred specifically to the value of developing the skill of inner hearing. Further, P3 stated that being able to hear the score "in my mind" was "necessary . . . before my part came in." P4 commented that "musicianship has overall [helped] my . . . inner hearing which has overall aided me for learning the Bach cantata." This reference to using one's mind to internally hear the score correlates with the idea of thinking intelligently in sound, as discussed in chapter 2.

4.4.2 Musical Memory

Musical memory was also a consistently highly ranked musicianship element, considered very relevant (four participants) and extremely relevant (eight participants) to the rehearsal and performance process. Three of the twelve participants (P1, P3, P5) made specific reference to a well-developed musical memory as a valuable skill that aided in their ability to memorize quickly and efficiently during the beginning learning stage to allow more time for the final musical polishing stage towards the end of the rehearsal process. As P5 stated: "Musical memory tasks helped with memorizing the piece quickly. Once it is memorized, we can work on making it beautiful." P3 said that melodic memory had been an important part of their preparation, which "consisted of listening to recordings of the part . . . memorizing the patterns [and] then visualizing" these melodic patterns on the score.

4.4.3 Sight-Singing

Sight-singing was considered somewhat relevant (one participant), very relevant (two participants), and extremely relevant (nine participants) during the rehearsal and performance process.

A third of the participants (P4, P5, P11, P12) made specific mention of sight-singing as being one of the most useful skills to have developed in musicianship classes. P4 stated that "in [the] early stages I was able to learn my parts due to . . . making use of my sight-singing skills," and P10 agreed that sight-singing "also played a key role in the learning." P12 summarized the value of sight-singing skills as "the most useful part of the musicianship class, especially when concerning the Bach cantata." These responses would suggest that being able to sight-sing enabled quicker and more efficient learning of the Bach cantata for many participants.

4.4.4 Intervals

The ability to identify intervals fluently and accurately was considered very relevant (five participants) and extremely relevant (seven participants) to the rehearsal and performance process. Five of the twelve participants (P2, P3, P4, P9, P11) referred to intervallic fluency. Four participants (P2, P3, P9, P11) mentioned solfa as a tool that helped their fluency and accuracy with intervals. P3 said, "Musicianship classes have guided me to remember melodic intervals and patterns and to even hear these in solfa." P9 also agreed that "the different scales and intervals with the use of solfa was extremely helpful in making the unexpected notes and scale passages in the [vocal] line more secure."

4.4.5 Solfège

Solfège (solfa) was considered somewhat relevant (two participants), very relevant (two participants), and extremely relevant (eight participants). Although two participants ranked solfège a little lower in importance than inner hearing, musical memory, sight-singing, and intervals, it is perhaps significant that ten of the twelve participants made specific reference to the usefulness of solfège skills during the rehearsal and performances stages of the Bach cantata. P10 observed that "solfa was incredibly useful as a tool in learning the work." P11 expanded on this, stating it was "extremely helpful in making the unexpected notes and scale passages in the [score] more secure." Further, P1 remarked that "solfège has assisted me in helping efficiently sight-read the pieces," and P2 supported the value of "solfa for accurate intonation, and interval/sight-reading made learning the pieces faster, easier and more accurate." P5 also stated that "solfa is useful to clarify pitches in tricky passages," and P9 said, "Skills such as solfa . . . made it significantly easier to learn as well as remember the cantata. I believe that I would not have achieved it as well or in the time without [this] skill." P12 commented, "The music wasn't really easy, mostly for the fact that the music wasn't completely homophonic, and it was difficult to hear my part. The solfa has helped me tremendously with sight-reading and learning my part quicker and more efficiently." P3 commented in this same vein: "Musicianship classes have guided me to . . . hear in solfa." Interestingly, by way of contrast, P7 observed that "as a violinist, I didn't use much solfège because I imagined the finger numbers which helped my intonation and memorization, but solfège is definitely a tool that I used when leading out in [choral] sectional rehearsals." Significantly, most participants acknowledged solfa as one of the fundamental musicianship tools that underpinned their ability, efficiency, and confidence in relation to all eight other musicianship elements listed in figure 5 above.

4.4.6 Triads

The ability to identify triads fluently and accurately was considered somewhat relevant (two participants), very relevant (four participants), and extremely relevant (six participants) during the rehearsal and performance process. The significance of triads for all participants can perhaps be better understood in the broader context of visual and aural harmonic analysis. P7 expressed the value of triads in this way: "Harmony, scales, and visual analysis were most helpful for me because of how Bach uses each vocal part. Tonal and formal analysis [were] very important to my practices because knowing which chord is coming next and how your part fits in (especially in the #7 chorale) helped me understand the functions of each part, chord, phrase, and section of the cantata." P9 also stated that triads were one of the skills that "made it significantly easier to learn as well as remember the cantata" and believed that they "would not have achieved it as well or in the time without these skills."

4.4.7 Bach Chorale

The Bach chorale "Jesu, deine Passion" chorale harmonization in E-flat major was one of three highly ranked musicianship elements that garnered a mixed response among participants. One participant indicated that the chorale was not relevant to them, while the other eleven participants considered it somewhat relevant (one participant), very relevant (four participants), and extremely relevant (six participants) during the rehearsal and performance process. Part of this mixed response could be attributed to the fact that three participants had not been part of musicianship classes and therefore had not undertaken an in-depth study of the chorale harmonization before performing the cantata. Another possible explanation was that some participants might have considered Bach's earlier choral harmonization in E-flat major not particularly relevant. Bach later used just the chorale melody in G major as the foundation of the much more harmonically sophisticated seventh movement of the cantata. P2's comment in support of the preliminary study of the Bach chorale indicated that it gave them a "good ability to understand and recognize every voice while singing your own [which] was very helpful." Pedagogically, if time had allowed, perhaps it would have been useful for participants to have undertaken an in-depth study of all the chorale settings in various keys to give a broader picture of why Bach perhaps chose to reharmonize this particular melody in the context of a choral fantasy movement in the cantata.

4.4.8 Diatonic Scales

The study of diatonic scales was another of three highly ranked elements that drew a more divided response. One participant indicated that the study of diatonic scales was not relevant to them, while the other eleven participants considered it somewhat relevant (one participant), very relevant (six participants), and extremely relevant (four participants). P9 stated that scales were one of the skills that "made it significantly easier to learn as well as remember the cantata" and believed that they "would not have achieved it as well or in the time without these skills." Significantly, P11 believed that "the different scales . . . with the use of solfa was extremely helpful [to] make the unexpected notes and scale passages in the bass line more secure." Overall, scales were considered to be more valuable than not.

4.4.9 Simple Time Rhythm

Simple time rhythm (i.e., the study of beat, rhythm, and meter in the context of simple time) was the remaining highly ranked musicianship element that garnered a mixed response among participants. One participant indicated that the study of simple time rhythm was not relevant to them, while the other eleven participants considered it somewhat relevant (two participants), very relevant (five participants), and extremely relevant (four participants), during the rehearsal and performance process. Two participants did refer to the connection between sight-reading rhythms, which they referred to as "following rhythms" (P3) and "clapping complex rhythms" (P5) during musicianship classes with the fact that strong rhythm reading skills "came in handy for sight-reading" during rehearsals.

4.4.10 Conclusion

In summary, the questionnaire responses given for question 9 would suggest that although there are nine overall highly rated musicianship elements—inner hearing, musical memory, sight-singing, intervals, solfège, triads, Bach chorale, diatonic scales, simple time rhythm—each participant appears to favor different elements as extremely important to them individually. Collectively, there appears to be a consensus across all participants that inner hearing, musical memory, sight-singing, and intervals are the four musicianship elements that stand out as being the most important due to their consistently high rating across all participants.

Additionally, the questionnaire responses for question 11 would suggest that solfège is the most valued skill in the musicianship toolbox that underpins the four highest-rated musicianship elements. Although the participants rated solfège slightly lower in relevance compared to inner hearing, musical memory, sight-singing, and intervals, solfège was the musicianship element that appears to have enabled the greatest efficiency to the learning process as the numerous comments in question 11 would suggest. The adjective "efficient" and its adverb "efficiently" were commonly referred to by most participants when describing the value of solfège in relation to inner hearing, musical memory, sight-singing, and intervals. As such, it was evident that participants perceived solfège to be an essential foundational musicianship skill that enabled them to more efficiently develop what they discerned to be the higher-order musicianship goals of inner hearing, musical memory, sight-singing, and intervals. Therefore, the fundamental purpose of solfège can be understood as a musicianship tool that enables functional meaning and efficiency of thought to the musical process of thinking intelligently in sound. Together the five musicianship elements—inner hearing, musical memory, sight-singing, intervals, and solfège—were identified as key themes for analysis in the focus group results.

4.5 FOCUS GROUP DISCUSSION

The focus group provided a fascinating Bach cantata post-performance debriefing together with all twelve participants. The discussion that ensued enabled an opportunity for further analysis and reflection on common themes that emerged in light of the questionnaire responses. Specifically, these themes will be discussed in direct relation to the following five musicianship elements—inner hearing, musical memory, sight-singing, intervals, and solfège—with particular emphasis on the importance of solfège as the solid foundation upon which the other four rest. Ensemble (one voice per part) will be discussed as an important theme that emerged from the focus group discussion, even though its significance was not evident from the questionnaire responses alone.

4.5.1 Inner Hearing

Solfège and its various uses permeated much of the focus group discussion. It was particularly evident that solfège was the underlying basis for the following analytical discussion in relation to inner hearing or thinking in sound. P9 believed that the ability to hear other vocal parts in solfège internally helped with knowing where and when to come in with their vocal part. There was also general agreement among participants that a lot of practice can happen silently in one's head. P5 commented that "the inner hearing thing is helpful" during rehearsals while the conductor is working with another section. Rather than disengaging during this time, they observed: "You can spend time figuring it out even though you are not singing out loud so you can utilize every moment of practice."

4.5.2 Musical Memory

Musical memory is something that quite a few participants agreed had just happened gradually and almost imperceptibly over time. This almost accidental memorization of the Bach cantata was candidly summarized by P9's response when they stated: "I'm not an actual vocal student and . . . when we had that [final] run-through and we could sing the whole thing by memory and in German, I was like 'What?' If you'd told me that at the beginning I would have been like 'No, 100 percent that is not going to happen,' but it did!"

P12 also declared: "I feel like I can sing every single line of the choir. I can sing the cello, viola, and violin parts and all the choir parts." P7 added: "That's the good thing about learning the music that well because you become so involved with it that it becomes part of you." P1 and P8 had both been unable to sing with the choir until the dress rehearsal on the performance day. P1 made the salient observation that "the choir was more settled because they knew it by memory. I could tell, I could feel [the choir was] really confident and really sure of [their] parts which was awesome." At this point, P8 nodded in agreement.

While solfège was not directly mentioned in relation to musical memory in the focus group discussion, it is clear that the use of the solfège was integral to many other musicianship elements that worked together to ensure a thorough preparation of the cantata. Further, this would suggest that this integrated musicianship approach enabled the participants to memorize the work so thoroughly.

4.5.3 Sight-Singing

Solfège also helped with sight-singing, particularly with securing the difficult vocal passages. A particular bass line in the seventh-movement chorale (b. 11–13) was especially difficult for the bass section to master mainly because it transitioned through a rapid succession of chords. One of the basses (P10) recalled that "it definitely helped having the strings there too. But man, that section was a killer." Another bass (P11) agreed that solfège definitely helped get all the "accidentals . . . in the right place." P8 admitted they were perhaps not as fast at looking at the score and singing immediately in solfa. However, they also remarked: "When I practiced by myself at home, parts I struggled with or intonation-wise I'd write the solfa in and just practice it like that and that helped." P12 similarly stated, "I always use solfa. That's the first and only tool I go to when I sight-read."

4.5.4 Intervals

Solfège appears to be directly foundational to intervallic reading fluency for P12, who acknowledged the connection like this: "Solfa and intervals, but I know intervals based on solfa. If I hear *do-fa*, then I know immediately what interval it is so that's what really helps me a lot." P3 acknowledged that "musicianship classes have guided me to remember melodic intervals and patterns and even hear these in solfa." P4 suggested that "in the early stages I was able to learn my parts due to identifying intervals" and believed that "knowledge of intervals . . . has overall aided me for learning the Bach cantata. When considering the relationship between solfa and intervals in the context of performing the Bach cantata, P3 believed that "some intervals were hard to simply memorize, therefore it was necessary to write solfa underneath and hear it in my mind before my part came in." P9 commented that having a secure working knowledge of intervals also "made it significantly easier to learn as well as remember the cantata." P11 thought that the intervallic work done in musicianship class "with the use of solfa was extremely helpful in making the unexpected passages in the bass line more secure."

4.5.5 Solfège

The relevance of solfège has been shown to inform the aforementioned musicianship elements. Solfège was also attributed to a variety of other musicianship elements that will be briefly considered here. The discussion touched on the use of tonic solfa or moveable *do* in relation to the skill of transposition by P12 with general agreement from all other participants. P2 observed that "our general understanding of a piece grows as a result of knowing solfa." P5 added to this by recalling that in musicianship class, when they were asked to sing the *do* or *la* of a piece, "it got a bit annoying, singing the *do* or *la* like . . . Why are we doing this? But now it's like you hear a song and you can just find the tonic." As an experienced musicianship pedagogue, I believe this is one of the most valuable attributes of the solfège (tonic solfa or moveable *do*) system. Functional meaning is embedded into each pitch in relation to all other pitches and particularly in relation to the tonic.

There was also reference made to the usefulness of solfège in regard to secure intonation. P1, who was an early-career music teacher, observed that solfège "fine-tunes your intonation as well" and had already "noticed in teaching that if you go over it in solfa and in letter names, the solfa is more secure. They know the interval is a fifth and they know what it sounds like. Whereas if you say to them, 'Sing C to G,' they are like 'Okay, um,' they are all over the place with it." This statement led to a friendly debate among the focus group participants as to which was more beneficial: singing in solfège or letter names. P7 was firmly in favor of letter names as a pitch reference point, which was primarily because they have absolute pitch. P7 found letter names strongly associated with absolute pitches and stated: "For me, it was more letter names. I still use solfa sometimes, but for me mostly because of the way that I was brought up from a younger age, it's always been letter names and finger numbers as a violinist . . . because I know all the pitches it goes straight into my head." Interestingly, P7 also made a comment in question 11 of the questionnaire that solfège "is definitely a useful tool that [they] used when leading out in sectional rehearsals." P7's comments are generally in keeping with common responses I have heard anecdotally over many years from my musicianship students and professional colleagues (string players in particular), who possess a well-developed sense of absolute pitch. They at first do not tend to see the usefulness of relative solfège because they already have a clear aural understanding of intervallic relationships memorized in their head. However, what many of my students and professional colleagues with perfect pitch do eventually come to understand and appreciate is the inner-hearing sense of extra-fine precision tuning of intonation that the use of relative solfège can help cultivate.

P7's position regarding letter names being more valuable than solfège was countered by P12, who said that they had been brought up from an early age with both solfège and letter names but "always preferred solfège . . . Letter names for me [are], like what [P7] mentioned, as a violinist I can see notes in finger numbers, but as a singer it is [in] different sections in my head. As a singer I always look at solfège. Letter names for some reason, except for when I'm trying to figure out something specific, [don't] really immediately register; it has to go through an extra step in my head." So, what is it about relative solfège that makes it incredibly useful? A few participants (P1, P10, P12) responded with the following similar answers: that it functions in any key; that it provides a "visual" representation of sound; that it is always "relative" to the tonic, so it's good for developing relative pitch; and that it is excellent for "fine-tuning intonation" as mentioned above.

Solfège also enabled some participants to learn quickly and efficiently. P1 stated: "When it comes to musicianship, how important it is to learn something so efficiently. This is not me bragging, so please don't take this the wrong way, but after a couple of years of practice I was able to look through it and sight-read it in my head using solfa because [the conductor] has equipped me with those skills. And I think if you guys keep practicing, you will be able to do that too if you can't already."

4.5.6 Ensemble (One Voice per Part)

Ensemble deserves a special mention as a significant theme that emerged in the focus group discussion. This musicianship element received an overall rating of 3.9, slightly below the 4.0 threshold from question 9 of the questionnaire and therefore not included as one of the musicianship elements discussed above. However, ensemble performance featured heavily in the focus group occupying approximately 20 percent of the discussion. P4 believed ensemble singing (one voice per part) helped develop the skill of listening to their own part against other parts. P2 made the insightful comment: "I find that performing and practicing in a small group really helps with being able to . . . perform with an understanding that you're actually a part of a piece developing in a unique structure of a piece. You are not just on your own. So, when you are singing or when you are performing . . . you have to have the other parts in mind in order for it to come together really well and when it does, and when each member has that, the piece takes off. It has a completely different dimension. That's what I feel as though the ensemble groups help us to do." P8 and P12 observed that ensemble singing with one voice per part increased their confidence, and P7 agreed by saying, "If all the parts are confident, then the whole group is going to sound confident."

On the historically informed performance question of whether Bach had originally intended the choral parts to be sung with just one voice per part, P7 made the perceptive observation that Bach had thankfully scored the orchestral string parts to double the vocal parts if one voice per part was to be considered. P1, P4, and P9 were undecided about whether singing one voice per part was even possible. This was mainly on the grounds of what they believed to be necessary teamwork required in relation to "scatter breathing" in order to maintain the musical integrity of the vocal line. Finally, P12 stated: "I found the discipline that develops having been in a small ensemble . . . there is a lot of responsibility on you to actually pull your weight and not to just kind of fall back on somebody who is a stronger leader. You are actually forced to be in charge of your own part, which helps a lot in choir and in any ensemble, even in your solo performance, it gives you more confidence [that] you can do it." Finally, solfège was quoted by several participants as having helped them immeasurably with sight-singing in the ensemble context. Specific reference was made to the use of solfège in relation to hearing one's part against the others and inner-hearing the part's place in the interval, chord, or key being sung or played.

4.6 CONCLUSION

Solfège is a goal of both the musicianship program and the rehearsal process. The participant responses to questions 9 and 11 of the questionnaire suggested that solfège is the fundamental musicianship element that underpins the development of the four highest-rated musicianship elements: inner hearing, musical memory, sight-singing, and intervals. Together these five elements, along with the addition of ensemble singing (one voice per part), formed the basis of the focus group discussion that again highlighted solfège as a foundational musicianship element. This is in keeping with the significant body of literature discussed in chapter 2 that asserts the pedagogical importance of a tonic-centric solmization system to musicianship skill development.

5

Results and Discussion: Recital 2 | Research Stage 2

If I have seen further,
it is by standing on the shoulders of giants.

Isaac Newton

5.1 RECITAL 2: GABRIEL FAURÉ, *REQUIEM*

THE SECOND RESEARCH STAGE examined my musicianship self-mentor preparation as a conductor through the rehearsal and performance process that culminated in my second doctoral recital. This recital comprised a live performance of Gabriel Fauré's *Requiem* together with a critical commentary and program notes highlighting aspects of historically informed performance practice relevant to this work.

5.2 RESEARCH STAGE 2: CONDUCTOR AS MUSICIANSHIP SELF-MENTOR

Research stage 2 occurred in conjunction with the second recital. The purpose of this second research stage was to focus on the conductor's role as musicianship self-mentor. In this paradigm, I am the conductor who functions as my musicianship self-mentor. Stage 2 research results were therefore gleaned from a self-reflective journal.

5.3 SELF-REFLECTIVE JOURNAL

The self-reflective journal documented the rehearsal and performance process from three different perspectives. The first perspective (part A) reflected on my role as understudy and assistant to Associate Professor Dr. Neil McEwan, artistic director and conductor of the Sydney Conservatorium of Music Choir and Chamber Choir, and my eventual role as guest conductor of these combined choirs. The second perspective (part B) reflected on the role of musicianship in my self-mentoring preparation as conductor for Gabriel Fauré's *Requiem*. The third perspective (part C) reflected on my role as understudy and guest conductor of the Sydney Conservatorium of Music Symphony Orchestra, which necessitated liaising closely with the orchestra's chief conductor, Maestro Eduardo Diazmuñoz. The self-reflective journal process unexpectedly brought to consciousness the possibility that there was also an informal peer mentoring relationship occurring simultaneously in the background, informing the foregrounded self-mentoring process. This emergent idea informs the ensuing three-part self-reflective journal discussion below.

5.3.1 Self-Reflective Journal: Part A Reflections

Excerpts from this first part of my self-reflective journal were selected for their ability to highlight my personal thoughts and ideas about the conductor as musicianship mentor (CMM) in the context of my initial role as assistant to Neil McEwan and my eventual role as guest conductor of the combined Sydney Conservatorium choirs. The key themes that have emerged from my self-reflective journal are highlighted in the following discussion.

From a musicianship perspective, three ideas were readily apparent. First, the level of musicianship skill ability each student brings to the choral rehearsal and performance space is varied. Musicianship skill development is integral to the undergraduate music program for music students who participate as singers in the Sydney Conservatorium Choir and Chamber Choir. However, not all members of each choir study music as their primary focus, as both choirs are open to audition, and any student at the University of Sydney may apply.

Second, one of my key roles as an assistant to McEwan was to take the vocal warm-up session at the beginning of choir rehearsals. I became increasingly more strategic in my planning of the vocal warm-up sessions in order to develop the kind of musicianship skills I thought would be complementary to the particular choral situation—specifically, where the two separate choirs would eventually merge to become one choir in the performance. This meant that musicianship exercises during vocal warm-up sessions were focused particularly on inner hearing in relation to intonation, balance, and blend as a priority. I intended to complement McEwan's work with each choir and enable ideal conditions for a homogenous sound when the two choirs later merged into one choir in the rehearsal and performance space.[1]

Third, it was generally accepted that a certain level of sight-singing ability was a prerequisite expectation for membership in either or both choirs. An adequate sight-singing ability was expected for the conservatorium choir, and a confident sight-singing ability was expected for the chamber choir. Nevertheless, the level of sight-singing ability was noticeably varied during the early stages of learning the repertoire in the first few rehearsals and more strikingly evident in some of the vocal sectional rehearsals that I

1. For a historical overview of the choral warm-up, see Dettwiler, "Developing Aural Skills."

was often assigned to lead. With limited rehearsal time available, it was the expectation that individual students with lower-level sight-singing ability would work harder away from the rehearsal in their own practice time to develop this skill quickly to cope with the sheer volume of music and the corresponding demands during rehearsal.

From a mentoring perspective, it slowly occurred to me that an informal peer mentor relationship between McEwan (my doctoral conducting supervisor) and myself had emerged alongside my self-mentoring as an additional mentoring outcome throughout the second research stage. While my self-reflective journal documented an overt awareness of my self-mentoring process, I came to realize, perhaps unsurprisingly, that my journal also revealed another layer of simultaneous mentoring from McEwan that occurred during this time. On reflection, what began as a mentee-mentor relationship ended as more of what I would term an informal peer-mentor relationship. I do recall that McEwan intentionally referred to me as his colleague during the early rehearsal stages of the Fauré *Requiem*, particularly when handing the choir over to me to rehearse on his behalf. This was a kind and generous referral that helped to instill the choir's confidence in my leadership during rehearsals, but also, more importantly, because I would be their conductor during the final performance.

This informal peer-mentoring relationship can also be reciprocal, but first, "a paradigm shift from 'maestro to mentor' needs to happen."[2] It became increasingly evident that I did have a slowly emerging sense of this paradigm shift in how I viewed McEwan from that of maestro-mentor to that of informal peer-mentor that began during the rehearsal process for the Fauré *Requiem*. Indeed, over the entire period of five years where McEwan was my official conducting supervisor for my doctoral degree, this shift was evident when considering the informal collegial professional relationship that now exists between McEwan and myself. The most important point to make here is that although the mentor-mentee relationship between McEwan and myself remained consistent

2. Castanheira, "Mentoring for Educators' Learning," 338.

throughout the doctoral journey, it was the nature of this relationship that shifted ever so slightly. This was evident by McEwan increasingly referring to me as his colleague even though I was still technically the conducting mentee student, and he was still the conducting mentor supervisor.

5.3.2 Self-Reflective Journal: Part B Reflections

Excerpts from part B of the self-reflective journal provide a comprehensive overview of the musicianship and conducting self-mentoring process I followed to prepare for my first performance of the Fauré *Requiem* as conductor of the Sydney Conservatorium Symphony Orchestra and Choirs.

The musicianship self-mentoring process I followed in my preparation of the Fauré *Requiem* was comprehensive, in-depth, and broad in purpose, requiring an intense intellectual focus together with a rigorous practice routine to ensure a thoroughly deep knowledge of the work as a whole, both the choral and conductor scores. This process utilized the musicianship skills valued by Guido d'Arezzo, Johann Sebastian Bach, and Nadia Boulanger, as discussed in chapter 2. They are also the same musicianship skills valued by my mentors over the past three decades and particularly during my two intense years of musicianship and conducting studies at the Liszt Academy's Kodály Institute in Hungary. The musicianship self-mentoring preparation process I learned and still utilize as a conductor is precisely the same preparation process I now model to my music students, expecting that this process will assist them in developing into self-mentors also at some point through the mentor-mentee process. In this way, the CMM model informs my own professional best practice and ensures the legacy continues through my students, past, present, and future.

5.3.3 Self-Reflective Journal: Part C Reflections

Excerpts from this third part of my self-reflective journal have been selected to highlight my role as understudy and guest conductor of the Sydney Conservatorium of Music Symphony Orchestra, which meant liaising closely at times with the orchestra's chief conductor, Eduardo Diazmuñoz. This brought about another brief, informal mentoring relationship.

From a conducting perspective, a further three ideas became apparent during my preparation. First, the highly disciplined approach I applied to the study of both the full orchestral and choral conductor scores for the Fauré *Requiem* was undoubtedly in no small part owing to the rigorous routine of musicianship training I had learned during my time as a student in both Hungary and Australia.

Second, my professional experience as a pianist was an extremely efficient way to help me prepare the vocal score and full conductor score. Well-developed musicianship skills like sight-singing and score reading at the piano enabled me to efficiently sing and play my way through the essential choral and orchestral score preparation process. This preparation process is discussed briefly in the reflections of part B above.

Third, one of the challenges of any conductor is to be thoroughly conversant with the orchestral instruments one is conducting. Although I had many years of experience working with wind, brass, and percussion musicians in an orchestral context, there is always more to learn about the individual nuances of each particular instrument. Fortunately, my considerable experience as a string player enabled an instant connection with at least two-thirds of the orchestra, which was a distinct advantage in this situation as the Fauré *Requiem* is heavily scored for strings, particularly the viola section.

As mentioned earlier in the journal discussions above, the rigorous musicianship self-mentoring process I followed in my preparation of the Fauré *Requiem* was essential to ensure I felt musically confident and secure at all rehearsals with the orchestra.

When I reflected on the part C journal entries, it is clear that by the time I met the orchestra, my thoughts were no longer consumed with the detailed musicianship process. A secure musicianship foundation gave me much-needed confidence as a conductor to know that I was well prepared musically and technically for this first meeting. Therefore, this enabled me to concentrate on other equally important logistical and administrative matters like rehearsal schedules and seating plans and to focus on important musical considerations during rehearsals, like setting tempos together with the orchestra, exploring expressive elements, and refining the overall balance of the orchestra internally between the sections and in relation to soloists and the choir.

In summary, the feeling of self-assurance that gradually emerged throughout my self-mentoring journal entries was due in no small part to the thorough musicianship preparation journey that I had undertaken. This may also explain why my self-reflective journal entries were increasingly brief towards the end of the rehearsal process; I was no longer preoccupied with these self-reflections as I was totally absorbed with the demands of the music in the moment. My self-reflective journaling had served its purpose in that this emerging element of confidence in my general overall feeling of preparedness had superseded the need to express any self-doubts or concerns in writing. At that moment, I was in my element in front of the orchestra and choir, secure in the knowledge that my musicianship was the sure foundation that enabled me to be my most authentic self as a conductor who brings the music to life.

The informal mentor relationship with Eduardo Diazmuñoz was distinctly different from that of Neil McEwan, as evidenced in my self-reflective journal. To me, Diazmuñoz remained the maestro, partly because that was his official title, but also because of the nature of my relationship to Diazmuñoz, which remained much more formal in my designated role as understudy and guest conductor for the Fauré *Requiem*. Diazmuñoz did alternate between mentor and colleague in his professional dealings with me. He was generous in his willingness for me to sit in on rehearsals so I could observe and get a general feel for working with the orchestra. He also kindly allowed me to sit in on various conducting master classes and workshops too. When it finally came time for me to work with the orchestra, Diazmuñoz actively mentored me on a few occasions at McEwan's request, through observing my conducting and rehearsal technique and giving me valuable feedback where necessary.

5.4 CONCLUSION

It is fitting to end this mentoring discussion with a quote by Bean et al. that emphasizes the valuable relational aspect of mentoring: "Mentoring is first and foremost a relationship. At its best mentoring can be a life-altering relationship that inspires mutual growth, learning, and development. Its effects can be remarkable, profound, and enduring; mentoring relationships have the capacity to transform individuals."[3] That my conducting mentor relationship with Neil McEwan was a significant factor in my development as a conductor cannot be underestimated. McEwan was ever the gentleman and while his diplomacy was much valued during the challenging moments of rehearsals, so too was his capacity to recognize, nurture, and champion my conducting abilities. In short, it was a genuinely transformational mentoring relationship.

Finally, self-reflective practice is a key feature of research stages 2 and 3. The notion of self-reflective practice and its value to the reflective practitioner originated with the work of Donald Schön in the 1970s. Schön argued that skilled practitioners demonstrate "reflection-in-action," which is essentially the process of "thinking what they are doing while they are doing it."[4] More recently, the influence of this original concept is evident in the work of scholars like David Elliott, who refers to "critically reflective engagement" as central to "reflective and creative practitioners" in his praxial philosophy of music education, and Linda Candy, who

3. Bean et al. "Mentoring in Higher Education," 57.

4. Schön, *Educating the Reflective Practitioner*, xi.

explores the concept of the reflective practitioner in the context of the creative process as discussed in her recently published work *The Creative Reflective Practitioner.* In the context of the second research stage, the conductor as self-mentor can be understood to assume this role of a critical, creative, and reflective practitioner.

6

Results and Discussion: Recital 3 | Research Stage 3

6.1 RECITAL 3: KARL JENKINS, *THE ARMED MAN: MASS FOR PEACE*

THIS THIRD RESEARCH STAGE examined the means by which the original mentees emerged as their own self-mentors through the rehearsal and performance process for the third doctoral recital. This recital comprised a live performance of Karl Jenkins's *The Armed Man: Mass for Peace* together with the program notes and a critical commentary highlighting creative performance aspects in relation to the Australian premiere performance of this work.

6.2 RESEARCH STAGE 3: CONDUCTOR'S MENTEES BECOME SELF-MENTORS

Research stage 3 occurred in conjunction with the third recital. The purpose of this third research stage was to focus on the conductor's mentees who had emerged as their own self-mentors over the two intervening years between the first and third recitals. In this paradigm, I am the conductor, and the participants in this research stage are some of my original mentees, who had since become independent self-mentors. Stage 3 research results were therefore gleaned from follow-up interviews with four of the original twelve participants. The research data for this third research stage were written responses from P4, P6, P7, and P12 in relation to a follow-up interview. These four participants were given the follow-up interview questions in the week leading up to the recital date, with instructions to consider the questions prior to the performance but to wait until after the recital before answering. Immediately following the performance, the four participants were encouraged to answer the questions as a post-performance reflection. With reference to the concluding comments in chapter 5, a parallel can be drawn with this stage of the study, as the participant self-mentors become critical, creative, and reflective practitioners. This reflective process is the wisdom of hindsight that informed the participants, and they brought this to the follow-up interview two years later.

6.3 FOLLOW-UP INTERVIEW

The follow-up interview was comprised of four questions. The first two questions were designed to highlight the ways in which mentees had become their own self-mentors. Question 1 was divided into four subsections and, together with question 2, asked participants to reflect over the intervening years between the first and third recitals. The remaining questions were designed to investigate the ways in which mentees might have also become emerging mentors. Question 3 focused on the participants who were in their fourth and final year of an undergraduate music education degree and who were about to begin their career as music teachers. Conversely, question 4 focused on the participants who were both recent music education graduates and early-career music teachers. Participants were asked to choose between questions 3 and 4 by answering the one that seemed more appropriate to their current circumstances.

6.3.1 Question 1A

Two years ago, you participated in the rehearsal and performance of a Bach cantata. Think back to that time and where your musicianship skills were. With reference to the following—solfège, letter names, intervals, intonation, inner hearing, establishing the tonic, transposition, ensemble, one voice per part,[1] conducting, clef reading, sight-singing—which particular musicianship skills have been the most beneficial to your personal musicianship development in relation to performance over the past two years, and why?

Two years earlier, during stage 1 of the research study, participants had been asked to rate all forty-six musicianship elements according to their perceived importance and to make brief comments about the most highly rated musicianship elements in relation to their perceived relevance to the rehearsal and performance process. The twelve musicianship elements listed in question 1A above had been selected from the forty-six musicianship elements listed in the original stage 1 questionnaire. Six elements (inner hearing, sight-singing,[2] intervals, solfège, ensemble, one voice per part) had been chosen for their highlighted significance from stage 1 analysis.[3] The other six musicianship elements (letter names, intonation, establishing the tonic, transposition, conducting, clef reading) had been included for their perceived significance by the researcher. It was my intention to draw respondents to comment specifically on four of the five elements from research stage 1 (solfège, inner

1. Ensemble and one voice per part are listed as two separate musicianship elements on the questionnaire and follow-up interview. However, participant responses suggest that they understand these terms as overlapping. Therefore, they will be referred to together.

2. Sight-reading and sight-singing are regarded as slightly different but overlapping skills, and participants' responses showed they understood them as interchangeable in this context.

3. One element highlighted in stage 1 analysis (musical memory) was not included again in research stage 3, as memorization of the score was not an expectation for the third recital performance.

hearing, sight-singing, and intervals) as well as encourage participants to comment on the additional eight elements included in this question. By purposely narrowing down the musicianship elements that could be commented on, it was hoped that participant responses would reveal a deeper, more mature understanding of their significance now that each participant was two years older and wiser.

These eight musicianship elements were commented on by at least two of the four participants as having been the most beneficial to their personal musicianship development in relation to performance over the past two years: inner hearing (P4, P6, P12), sight-singing (P6, P7, P12), intervals (P4, P6, P12), solfège (P4, P6, P12), ensemble/one voice per part (P4, P6, P12), intonation (P4, P6, P12), letter names (P6, P7), and conducting (P4, P6). Of the other three musicianship elements, one (establishing the tonic) was referred to by one participant and will be commented on briefly. The remaining two (clef reading, transposition) were not referred to and therefore not included for further discussion.

P4 wrote about how these musicianship skills had been transformational in relation to their individual ability to sing confidently in public: "The work I put into the Bach cantata has been pivotal for me in choral singing . . . the huge development that I have had in these areas of my musicianship have dramatically increased my confidence of publicly singing." P4 also stated that ensemble singing with one voice per part "really developed my intonation" and "understanding how to conduct" had "really helped [them] in rehearsals."

P6 was aware that their musicianship skills had "very much developed over the past two years," stating that when first starting to learn the Bach cantata, "I liked to rely on skills that I had become more familiar with." For example, learning vocal parts by first playing the vocal line on the flute to help "hear my voice part . . . however, I have since developed my skills in more areas through musicianship classes," and emphasized that "having the time to have information sink in and develop" over the two years was vitally important. They could "now see the interval and hear it within" themselves (i.e., inner hearing) and "often used solfège as an extra backup," which made "sight-reading more fluent." P6 mentioned that the ensemble singing with one voice per part "really helped to ensure that I had learnt it well . . . and you know exactly how to sing your part which may be harder [to do] on your own." P6 also credited ensemble singing one voice per part with improved intonation. They observed: "Hearing your part in context is always helpful for intonation . . . I am more confident in my intonation and am now aware of the intonation of others around me." With reference to conducting, P6 commented: "I knew how to follow the score but would occasionally get lost for various reasons. I find now that I am paying more attention and asking more questions about what the conductor is doing to [more confidently] follow along." P6's response would suggest that their emerging confidence is directly proportional to their level of musicianship ability, evident from the development that occurred between the first and third recitals when compared. P6 said that "having the time to [let the] information sink in and develop" was invaluable to their overall musicianship skills. This is undoubtedly a very pleasing response from the perspective of a musicianship mentor. From the conductor's perspective, the greater the musicianship of each individual, the greater efficiency in the rehearsal process, and the greater the level of musicality attainable from the ensemble as a whole.

P7 made brief observations that centered primarily on sight-reading skills. They believed that "using letter names was the best way of practice" for them but also acknowledged that "solfège came in handy with the trickier intervals." P12, by way of contrast, believed that sight-reading using solfège and interval recognition "definitely made the whole process faster" when needing to learn repertoire quickly. P12 then commented on the experience of singing in ensembles with one voice per part in the rehearsal context: "Once I knew my part, the real challenge lay in being able to sing with other voices within an ensemble without losing the sense of intonation or 'togetherness,' so having those skills previously developed throughout my musicianship training [was] very beneficial." Interestingly, P12 had been the one designated to give starting pitches during vocal rehearsals and comments positively about the development of this valuable skill: "During the rehearsal of Bach's cantata, I was also in charge of giving the correct starting pitches for the ensemble by just using a tuning fork tuned to A440. Therefore, the interval recognition skills and the ability to establish a tonic made the whole process easier and less stressful." P12's comments indicate a level of confidence directly proportional to the security of their musicianship skill development.

A significantly notable correlation evident in the overall responses to question 1A is the fact that of the eight musicianship elements commented on, four of them (inner hearing, sight-singing, intervals, and solfège) were also in the five highest-ranked musicianship elements gleaned two years earlier from the stage 1 questionnaire. Each of these four elements was referred to by at least three out of the four participants. Participant comments regarding ensemble singing with one voice per part suggest that an already established confidence in this ability is invaluable, particularly because these participants were learning their individual parts quite independently away from the ensemble.

Taken as a whole, participant's responses to this question indicate overall confidence in their individual and collective ability to prepare "quickly" and "faster" because of their musicianship skills which "made the whole process easier and less stressful," according to P12. The two-year time period between the first and third recitals is likely an essential ingredient in developing overall confidence in each of the four participants, whose responses collectively suggest that the depth and breadth of musicianship skills developed over time.

6.3.2 Question 1B

Thinking forward, which particular musicianship skills would be most beneficial to your ongoing personal musicianship development in relation to performance in the future, and why?

P4 highlighted intonation, intervals, conducting, and sight-singing as the four most useful skills and made the following interesting observation: "I find that conducting myself in rehearsal helps me give expression to the music." P6 emphasized the fact that all musicianship skills would "forever help me in my musicianship development," but thought solfège, intervals, and intonation were the most important of these skills for the future. They emphasized the continued importance of "working with different ensembles and conducting" because of the perceived opportunity to "further develop my skill . . . and expose me to new works that I may not have chosen myself, forcing me to use all my skills to deliver what is required." P7 reiterated the usefulness of solfège for trickier intervals (e.g., diminished and augmented) but stated that their "primary practice will still be sight-singing and letter names" because of their "training as a violinist." P12 said the skills considered most beneficial at present were solfège and sight-singing skills but, like P6, agreed that all skills would be "beneficial to my ongoing musicianship development" because of plans to become a music teacher. One would hope that this same self-awareness may also mean that participants will continue to value their musicianship skill development as professional music educators when passing these skills to their students.

Overall, solfège and sight-singing were the musicianship elements most commented on, with three out of the four participants referring to the usefulness of these two elements, and solfege being the foundation on which fluent sight-singing skills are built, according to P4, P6, and P12. By contrast, P7, who is an instrumentalist first and foremost, highlights fluency in both solfège and letter names as the dual foundation upon which their sight-singing skills are built. This is consistent with the results from research stage 1, in which these two musicianship elements—solfège and sight-singing—were highly rated in the questionnaire and mentioned significantly in the focus group discussion.

6.3.3 Question 1C

Reflect on the synergy between musicianship class and the Bach cantata rehearsal and performance process. How meaningful was it to study the Bach cantata repertoire in musicianship class during the rehearsal and performance process, and why?

P4 remarked: "I found it very interesting looking at the Bach cantata in-depth during musicianship classes. I found the harmonic analysis we did assisted me in performance by hearing the harmonic progressions and hence made it much easier to hear starting notes." P6 further elaborated: "I thoroughly enjoyed studying the Bach cantata repertoire in class. It gave me a deeper knowledge and appreciation for the context and execution of each section, not only in ways that my conductor wished for but in ways that perhaps [historically] Bach may have wanted as well." P7 commented that "studying Bach during class and rehearsals was very beneficial as we were beginning to understand what Bach was trying to accomplish in his musical word painting and the relationship which he always brings out between the orchestra and the choir." P12 observed:

> I believe that by studying the Bach cantata during the musicianship class, I was able to get a more in-depth approach to learning the piece. We learned the meaning of the words in greater detail, learned all the parts of the cantata, so we were aware of other voice lines other than our own, and we also had the chance to apply the cantata in different and creative ways (e.g., improvisation on the main theme, changing the cantata to a minor key, etc.) which ultimately helped in retaining the cantata for a longer period of time.

Some of these comments in response to question 1C are interesting because they hint at each participant's growing awareness of historically informed performance (HIP) practice. Indeed, performing the Bach cantata in a historically informed way was one of my focus points as a conductor in preparing the score and as a mentor when preparing the vocalists and instrumentalists during the rehearsal and performance process. Although HIP aspects were not the central focus of the first recital, I was genuinely pleased that awareness of HIP approaches was present in the participant responses and significant enough for them to have commented on two years later.

These responses suggest that all four participants believed their in-depth study of the Bach cantata during musicianship class, in parallel with the rehearsal of the Bach cantata, allowed for a richer, more profound, integrated learning experience overall. P4 and P12 commented positively about the in-depth approach, while P6 and P7 referred to a deeper understanding of Bach's cantatas and a new appreciation of HIP practices regarding the Baroque era.

Musicianship and ensemble performance happen to be two components that sit side by side in several music units of study through the Avondale Conservatorium. This decision to pair these two components was both a practical and pedagogical one at the time. However, with the wisdom of hindsight, this pairing has also allowed the opportunity for incredible synergistic learning to take place at the nexus between musicianship and ensemble performance. This synergy allows for a richer and more holistic teaching and learning experience for the participants and their conductors and musicianship mentors.

When comparing and contrasting the Bach cantata experience to the Jenkins *Armed Man* experience, quite obviously, the pedagogical scaffolding deliberately used to guide the participants through the Bach cantata by the conductor and musicianship mentor was no longer in place for the participants who performed the Jenkins work two years later. However, what is interesting to note is that without their reliance on a mentor to provide the scaffolding, they had become their own self-mentors, providing their own self-directed learning. They had absorbed enough of the routines, discipline, habits, and training required to acquire the musicianship skills to become confident and efficient self-mentors.

Thus, the synergy between the musicianship class and the Bach cantata rehearsal and performance process would appear to have allowed for a deeper and more meaningful learning experience for participants, particularly in the area of historically informed performance practice, and eventually led to self-directed learning during the rehearsal and performance process for the Jenkins *Armed Man* two years later.

6.3.4 Question 1D

Reflect on the synergy between conducting class and the Bach cantata rehearsal and performance process. How meaningful was it to study the Bach cantata repertoire in conducting class during the rehearsal and performance process, and why?

All participants were expected to participate in a conducting class as part of the musicianship program. P4 was a beginner conductor and made the following observations: "Through the conducting class, I felt like I learnt all vocal parts in various pieces in the cantata inside out. Being able to hear the other parts and know what they were doing in the performance helped my intonation and rhythmic accuracy." P6's response is rather insightful, perhaps because as a principal study vocalist, their primary role in conducting class was to sing the bass recitative and aria for each student conductor. P6 elaborated:

> I found the conducting component the most helpful. It showed me how to use the techniques studied from musicianship class in practice, and that everyone does have their own interpretation of how pieces should be performed. They are not bad or wrong, some just made more sense than others. I was the performance soloist for our conducting class during this time. Singing the bass [recitative and] aria repeatedly for each student to perform their conducting style gave me insight to these nuances but also experienced the way in which they felt. It also solidified why my conductor wanted to present her performance in the way that she did.

P7 believed that "conducting class helped us understand where the entries for each part are. All of the choruses in this cantata are fugal in nature, so to be able to look through the full score, and to conduct it ourselves, made that a very handy rehearsal tool when it came to individual practice and the rehearsals." P12 did not comment, as they had not been present in the conducting class.

Ironically, around the time of the cantata performance, I do remember being increasingly aware that some participants might have reached a saturation point because J. S. Bach and his cantata had been the concentrated focus of both musicianship and conducting classes and of choral and orchestral ensemble rehearsals for almost the entire thirteen weeks of the semester. Despite my reservations, these responses would suggest all participants appeared to reflect positively on the opportunity to undertake a thorough study of various elements of the Bach cantata in both musicianship and conducting classes. Upon reflection, it would have been good to have counterbalanced the steady Bach cantata diet with the occasional and timely addition of contrasting repertoire and associated activities, perhaps as a circuit breaker and just for sheer enjoyment rather than for pedagogical outcomes.

Overall, the synergy between conducting class and the Bach cantata rehearsal and performance process was perceived to be a very positive learning experience that contributed to a deeper understanding of the cantata as a whole for all participants.

6.3.5 Question 2

You have been a participant in the rehearsal and performance process of Karl Jenkins's "The Armed Man: Mass for Peace," but you are no longer a musicianship and/or conducting student at Avondale. Therefore, you were not required to simultaneously do an intense, guided study of this work in musicianship and/or conducting class during the rehearsal and performance process. With this in mind, are there any acquired musicianship and/or conducting skills that you found particularly helpful in your individual, independent, personal preparation for this performance?

First, as with question 1A, inner hearing, intervals, and solfège were again the musicianship skills frequently referred to by three out of the four participants as the most helpful in their personal preparation. Second, this question was designed to tease out the individual, independent, personal preparation process for each participant. When all four participant responses were taken as a whole, the overarching theme that emerged was that the foundational musicianship and conducting skills established and developed while they were students in musicianship and conducting classes had now become a habitual part of their own personal preparation process. Two years later, these skills, and the habits of practice that formed in association with their development, continued to contribute to each participant's ability to be thoroughly prepared. From the comments made by each of the four participants, it is clear that they had matured in their attitude and confidence in relation to their self-directed learning during the rehearsal and performance process.

P4 stated: "I found with all the background listening I was doing [that] I became very familiar with the pieces and hence found it easy to learn my parts." P6, when faced with a particular musical challenge during rehearsals, felt confident that they had the necessary skills to solve it, stating: "It was the work I had done previously that helped with that transition." P7 commented on how their musicianship and conducting skills had been utilized "leading a sectional practice with the tenors" and also about how "having a prior performance knowledge of the music and being able to relearn it was very helpful too." P12 talked about an established learning pattern that utilized the musicianship skills developed as a student. This established learning pattern, although unique to each participant, is common to all four participants and appeared to be modelled directly from the routines established during their time as musicianship and conducting students in my classes. As I was their original mentor two years earlier for the Bach cantata, this realization was exactly what I had hoped for; to know that my role as mentor was all but redundant because the mentees had now become their own self-mentors.

So, while three musicianship elements—inner hearing, intervals, solfège—were highlighted, they were not the focus of each participant's discussion. Rather, each participant gave a much broader view of what was most important, which was that their own personal preparation process had been positively influenced by habits formed during musicianship class two years earlier that had developed into a reliable self-mentoring process.

6.3.6 Question 3

Reflect on your overall involvement in the musicianship and/or conducting program in relation to performance here at Avondale. In your experience as a final-year undergraduate music education student and pre-service teacher can you please comment on how you anticipate your involvement in the musicianship and/or conducting program in relation to performance has prepared you for a beginning career as a music teacher.

Participants were instructed to answer this question if they were a final-year undergraduate music education student and about to become an early-career music teacher. One response to this question was received (from P6), while P4, P7, and P12 declined.

While reflecting on their involvement in the musicianship, conducting, and performance aspects of the undergraduate music program, P6 was well aware that these aspects had prepared them for a beginning career as a music teacher. This was evident in their response: "The musicianship and conducting courses have helped develop my skills for teaching immensely. They . . . not only [gave] me the tools to analyze and understand the music I perform for myself but [also gave] me the confidence to find and teach these techniques to my students." P6 made specific reference to four musicianship elements consistently ranked highly in research stage 1, namely, solfège, intervals, conducting, and inner hearing. In P6's own words:

> I have had the privilege to use some of these skills in schools already on my placements with conducting bands and choirs. My teachers were impressed at the skills I had already developed and excited by some of the tools I used myself to teach to the students . . . they were not only proof to the students and my supervisor that I knew what I was doing but that I knew what I wanted to have these ensembles accomplish.

P6 mentioned these elements as integral to their increased sense of self-confidence during practice-teaching placements, particularly in their interactions with their supervising teachers and within the learning and teaching environment. P6's comments would suggest that a secure musicianship skill foundation gives confidence to final-year practice teachers and early-career music teachers and is an asset that has the potential to keep appreciating over a lifetime.

P6's response is insightful, particularly when viewed through the lens of the CMM model, first outlined in chapter 3. In this model, the research objective of stage 3 was twofold: to examine the process by which mentees become self-mentors and to examine the process by which mentees may become mentors to others. Concerning this twofold objective, P6's response to question 3 would suggest that they were both confident in their ability to self-mentor and increasingly aware of their transition from mentee to mentor, in parallel with their transition from final-year music education student to an emerging music teacher. Reid, Rowley, and Bennett explore this increased awareness of "sense of self" identity in relation to the gradual transformation from undergraduate music education student (current self) towards professional music educator (future self).[4] Viewed in this paradigm, P6's "sense of

4. See Reid et al., "From Expert Student," 402.

self" identity is growing in confidence as a final-year music education student transitioning into an early-career music teacher.

6.3.7 Question 4

Reflect on your progression from an undergraduate mentee student in musicianship and conducting in relation to performance at Avondale to an early-career teacher who has now become a mentor to your own students. Can you please comment on how you believe you have grown from mentee to mentor over the past two years, particularly in the area of musicianship and/or conducting in relation to performance?

Question 4 made specific reference to the transition from mentee to mentor and asked participants to comment on this transition. Participants were encouraged to answer this question if they were a recent music education graduate and an early-career music teacher. Two responses to this question were received from P4 and P7, while P6 and P12 declined to answer this question.

P4 explained this transition from mentee to mentor in several important ways. First, by recognizing the inherent value of musicianship skill development as a mentee undergraduate music education student, and later as a mentor in the professional teaching and learning environment: "In the last two years of my degree, I learnt the importance of developing my musicianship skills to the best of my ability, as it then lets my students have the access to the best possible learning." Second, P4 also realized the importance of seeking ongoing development opportunities in support of the teaching and learning environment: "I have had more access to musicianship and conducting classes through professional development opportunities that I have been completing to make sure my musicianship stays at a high level and does not fall to the current level of my students." Third, P4 recognized the personal and professional need to remain a practicing musician by continuing to seek out opportunities to perform: "I have also found that maintaining opportunities to perform works such as *The Armed Man* has also given me that added benefit of engaging in musical activities outside of the classroom. Taking part in these opportunities also gives me the chance to show to my students that I'm not just a music teacher, I'm a musician." Third, this comment highlights the importance of P4's growing confidence in their emerging identity as an early-career music teacher. P4 believed that conducting opportunities also enabled them to develop from mentee to mentor: "I am using my conducting skills more than ever in my classes and in my infant choir. The progress I have made in conducting has given me the confidence that I am a conductor in a regular classroom too." Finally, P4 stated that they are "so grateful for the training I have had through my degree, especially in the areas of musicianship and conducting. I feel that it has extended me past the requirements of an average music teacher and has given me the confidence to be the best teacher I can be." This highlights the importance of formal musicianship and conducting training in the higher music education context to ensure students are ready for a professional environment.

As a recent music education graduate and early-career music teacher, P7 was able to answer question 4 by looking objectively from the perspective of both the mentee and the mentor:

> From a mentee's perspective, [the conductor] demonstrated to us what it takes to gain a full understanding of a piece through our rehearsals and classes. Having the role of a mentor demonstrated in front of us knowing that one day we would become music mentors was invaluable to have. Learning how to effectively use the practice techniques (sight-reading, solfège intonation practice, self-conducting practice, analyzing the score etc. . . .) and sharing of basic vocal techniques is something that I want to use in my professional role now as a music mentor myself. As a leader of the tenor section this time around . . . I was able to put these points into practice during our sectionals and smaller group practices (soloists especially) and I was using the same

> practice techniques that [the conductor] taught me; and they worked very well with the group that I was rehearsing with.

Like P4's earlier response, this comment above from P7 suggests that they, too, exhibit increased confidence in their abilities commensurate with their emerging identity as a more advanced early-career music teacher.

Therefore, participants' responses would suggest that musicianship and conducting skill development are essential components in the undergraduate learning environment to ensure a smooth transition to an early-career music teacher. As participants grew in confidence, so did their ability to see themselves as having progressed from mentee to mentor.

6.4 CONCLUSION

During the third recital, I saw my mentees take an important step towards self-mentoring. Our rehearsal on the afternoon of the performance ran late. My other role of producing the concert was also placing last-minute logistical demands on me, so I decided we would rehearse the final number, "God Shall Wipe Away All Tears," later that day. I must admit we never did that because it slipped my mind. And so I walked on stage, took a bow, and commenced my final recital, where I was in my professional element, feeling the calm excitement of flow.[5] All went well until I turned the last pages of the score and saw "God Shall Wipe Away All Tears," with which Jenkins ends *The Armed Man*. This was the climax of the whole work, and only then did I realize we had not rehearsed it together! I looked at the faces of participants I had closely mentored over the past two years. They were smiling. I took a deep breath and maintained composure. Looking calm, they followed my instructions to stand. I lifted my hands, and they sang beautifully. All anxiety left me, and I fought back joyful tears while conducting. In the green room afterwards, they proudly told me: "We knew you were

5. See Robinson, *Element*; Csikszentmihalyi, *Flow*.

busy, so we formed our own rehearsal without you. We trusted you to lead us, and we knew you trusted us to sing. We knew what you would expect, so we were confident that we would be just fine when you lifted your hands." I realized my mentees were now self-mentoring, and my work as conductor and musicianship mentor was done. The baton had indeed been handed on.

7

Conclusion

THIS STUDY BEGAN WITH three research questions that explore the conductor as musicianship mentor (CMM) model. The answers that emerged will be summarized below. Limitations of the research and recommendations for further study will be considered before concluding comments.

7.1 WHAT IS THE ROLE OF THE CONDUCTOR AS A MUSICIANSHIP MENTOR?

The first research question investigated the role of the CMM to mentees in relation to recital 1. It was shown that the conductor was able to assist the participant mentees in the capacity of a musicianship mentor throughout the rehearsal and performance process. The conductor and musicianship mentor were the same person, which is significant in relation to the results of this study.

The results suggest first that mentees understood the musicianship mentoring role of the conductor as being particularly significant to their progress through the rehearsal and performance of the Bach cantata. Second, the questionnaire and focus group discussion identified the fact that participants were in general agreement about five specific musicianship elements that they considered were of greatest significance (inner hearing, musical memory, sight-singing, intervals, and solfège) throughout the rehearsal and performance process. These elements, along with many others, were incorporated pedagogically by me as their musicianship mentor, as well as their conductor. Third, most participants perceived solfège as the musicianship element that was most foundational to the development of the others. And fourth, there is reason to reflect on the ideal circumstances that enabled an authentic teaching and learning environment, where an intentional integration between the musicianship, conducting, solo performance, and ensemble performance program was able to occur. Such is the beauty of the synergy that occurs when academic music performance programs can be effectively integrated for the ultimate benefit of powerfully authentic teaching and learning experiences.

7.2 WHAT IS THE CONDUCTOR'S PERSONAL SELF-MENTOR PREPARATION?

The second research question explored the role of the conductor as a self-mentor in relation to the second recital. During this research stage, I consulted a broad range of conducting pedagogy literature to gain a deeper understanding of the personal self-mentoring preparation process of other conductors.[1] The process of self-mentoring was recorded in a reflective journal, later divided into three parts according to the three aspects of the preparation process. Part A reflected upon the process of working with Neil McEwan to prepare the mass choir, while part B reflected upon the musicianship self-mentoring process in relation to score preparation. Part C reflected upon the process of working with Eduardo Diazmuñoz to prepare the symphony orchestra.

1. Brown, *Classical & Romantic Performance*; Conlon, *Wisdom, Wit, and Will*; Emmons and Chase, *Prescriptions for Choral Excellence*; Holst, *Conducting a Choir*; Moses et al., *Face to Face*; Seaman, *Inside Conducting*; Thackar, *Principles of Conducting*.

Part A of the journal highlighted the development of the mentor-mentee relationship between myself and my conducting supervisor (McEwan) into an unofficial peer mentoring relationship throughout a two-year period between the first recital and the third recital. I became increasingly aware of this shift in dynamics, particularly when I was self-mentoring during my preparation for the second recital. Mentoring at its core is about relationships, and requires significant investment in people. I experienced gradual transformation in my relationship with my mentor, which was built on mutual trust. I trusted him as a mentor to guide me as a mentee, and in return, he trusted me as a mentee to do my best to follow his guidance. At first, we consulted together on every detail, but as my competence developed, so did his trust. Over time he was increasingly generous with his suggestions that we do things more collaboratively, and eventually, he treated me more like a peer. In contrast, part C of the journal indicated that the mentor-mentee nature of my professional relationship with Eduardo Diazmuñoz was established and remained that way during a relatively short three-month period.

As discussed in part B of the journal, score preparation required a rigorous approach to learning the full conductor score and vocal score to prepare thoroughly enough to rehearse and eventually conduct the choir and orchestra. As I began to undertake this score preparation process, I was immediately appreciative of the many years of rigorous training in musicianship skills that developed the personal and professional discipline required to be absolutely secure in my ability to be fully prepared to direct the choir and orchestra. Undoubtedly, it was the musicianship foundations that were laid, and associated habits that were formed, during my formative years in Australia and Hungary that gave me the confidence to operate independently as a professional musician.

7.3 WHICH MUSICIANSHIP SKILLS HAVE FORMER MENTEES RETAINED?

The third research question examined how the conductor's mentees from recital 1 became their own self-mentors in the context of their individual preparation for the third recital. The results suggest, first, that the musicianship skills considered most important to self-mentoring participants in the third research stage were inner hearing, sight-singing, intervals, and solfège. When participants were asked to suggest which musicianship element(s) would be most beneficial overall for the future, solfège and sight-singing were unanimously cited. Significantly, participants commented on the fact that solfège was fundamental to their development of sight-singing skills. Second, another musicianship element emerged in these research results: ensemble singing with one voice per part. Third, it was also apparent to the four participants that, just like my own realization in the second research stage, they had acquired the necessary musicianship skills to enable self-mentoring in their own personal preparation process. Finally, three of the four participants were able to recognize and articulate that not only had they become their own self-mentors but that they had also emerged as mentors in their own right, as either final-year music education students with significant teaching experience in the classroom or as early-career music teachers who were well on their way to becoming mentors to their mentee students. The two years between the first and third recitals witnessed participants transition from mentee to self-mentor and then to mentor of others. This is a powerful testimony to the fact that a pedagogically sequential musicianship skill development program, closely integrated with a strong ensemble performance program, can lay the foundations for mentee musicians to develop healthy professional self-mentoring and, eventually, mentoring habits for a lifetime.

7.4 LIMITATIONS OF THE STUDY

This study was limited to a relatively small sample size (n=12) and took place at a small higher education institution in a regional location, focusing largely on one demographic. All participants were of a roughly similar age (twenty to twenty-six years), and all except one had been through school in Australia, though a number had foreign-born parents: three Croatian, one Serbian, and one Vietnamese. All participants had been students in my musicianship and conducting classes, small vocal ensembles, and large choirs at various times and stages of their musical development at Avondale. At the time of this study, eleven participants were music education students, and the twelfth participant later progressed to further undergraduate study in music education. A control group for comparison was not used, and the potential for false positives and data bias is acknowledged. A broader engagement with conducting, musicianship, and singing pedagogy should have been considered; however, word limits restricted their inclusion. The repertoire used was representative of the Western art music canon, specifically the late Baroque, late Romantic, and contemporary periods. All three works were scored for orchestra and choral forces of various permutations. The Bach cantata was scored for vocal soloists with chamber choir and chamber orchestra, the Fauré *Requiem* was scored for soloists with mass choir and large symphony orchestra, and Jenkins's *The Armed Man: Mass for Peace* was scored for vocal soloists, large choral forces, and a large wind orchestra.

7.5 RECOMMENDATIONS FOR FURTHER RESEARCH

There is the opportunity for similar studies with different scopes to show the value of deliberately and overtly integrating musicianship into conducting, solo performance, and ensemble performance programs within the context of higher music education institutions, both in Australia and overseas.

To explore further the methodological model of CMM, similar research questions could be asked of a larger sample size, and projects could select participants from rural, suburban, and urban higher music education institutions. They could also consider different demographics and further comparative contexts. The potential for false positives may benefit from comparison with broader institutional course evaluation policies.

More specifically, this research methodology could be expanded to include a broader engagement with conducting, musicianship, and singing pedagogy. It could also be adapted more broadly to mentoring in the context of music education and more specifically to explore how conductors can mentor students on aspects of conducting other than musicianship, including conducting technique,[2] rehearsal technique,[3] and conducting score preparation.[4]

7.6 CONCLUDING COMMENTS

The role of the CMM in the interaction between a musicianship program that utilizes the Kodály concept of pedagogically sequential musicianship skill development with singing at its core and an ensemble performance program within the context of an Australian higher music education institution formed the basis for this research study. Musicianship training in higher music education programs is often a discrete, stand-alone study and assumes that the skills developed will be automatically transferred to the performance context.[5] However, this may not always be the case. This

2. See Jordan, *Evoking Sound: Fundamentals*; Galkin, *History of Orchestral Conducting*; Green and Gibson, *Modern Conductor*; Hart, "Music Education Conducting Curricula."

3. See Jordan, *Evoking Sound: Choral Rehearsal*, vol. 1; "Rehearsing the Orchestra," 39–44, in Moses et al., *Face to Face*.

4. See A. Jones et al., "Analyzing the Choral-Orchestral Score"; "Studying the Scores," 47–58, in Moses et al., *Face to Face*; Seaman, *Inside Conducting*, 155–200; Jordan, *Evoking Sound: Choral Rehearsal*, vol. 2.

5. See Karpinski, *Aural Skills Acquisition*, vii.

research study was conducted with students whose undergraduate music study program explicitly applied musicianship skills to the ensemble performance context, since I had the opportunity to teach foundational, intermediate, and advanced musicianship levels in parallel to the ensemble performance program. This research study suggests that a musicianship program with strong connections to a performance program allows for seamless integration and contributes significantly to the breadth and depth of learning. Intentionally integrating a pedagogically sequential musicianship skill development program that emphasizes singing into the rehearsal and performance process is richly rewarding and highly beneficial to the creation of an authentically synergistic learning environment for the conductor as mentor and the students as mentees. The most frequent comment I received when presenting this research project at conferences can be paraphrased as: "Aren't you lucky that you can integrate all of these aspects so well?" Indeed, the ability to integrate purposefully the higher music education curriculum in this way has made the learning environment more holistic, giving students the invaluable opportunity to combine study with experience through a practical performance of the work studied. It is an accepted fact that musicianship skill development is essential in a higher music education program. As this study discovered, when those musicianship skills are directly related to the performance of a studied work, they have the potential to become much more embedded and effective overall.

Bibliography

Allaire, Gaston G. *The Theory of Hexachords, Solmisation and the Modal System: A Practical Application*. Edited by Armen Carapetyan. Vol. 24 of *Musicological Studies and Documents*. Dallas: American Institute of Musicology, 1972.

Alperson, Philip. "Music Education." In *The Routledge Companion to Philosophy and Music*, edited by Theodore Gracyk and Andrew Kania, 614–23. London: Taylor & Francis, 2011.

Alter, Robert. *The Wisdom Books: Job, Proverbs, and Ecclesiastes*. New York: Norton, 2011.

Augustine, St. "Confessions." In Strunk, *Source Readings in Music History*, 2:132–33.

Bach, Johann Sebastian. *Chorale-Gesänge*. Edited by Bernhard F. Richter. Breitkopf 3765. Wiesbaden: Breitkopf & Härtel, n.d.

———. *Kantate Nr. 182: Himmelskönig, sei wilkommen*. BWV 182. Breitkopf 7182. Leipzig: Breitkopf & Härtel, n.d.

Barbera, André. "Pythagoras." Grove Music Online, 2001; last updated Feb. 11, 2013. https://doi.org/10.1093/gmo/9781561592630.article.22603.

Barker, Andrew. "Music." In *The Oxford Classical Dictionary*, edited by Simon Hornblower and Antony Spawforth, 975–85. 4th ed. Oxford: Oxford University Press, 2012.

Basil, St. "Homily on the First Psalm." In Strunk, *Source Readings in Music History*, 2:121–23.

Bean, Nadine M., et al. "Mentoring in Higher Education Should Be the Norm to Assure Success: Lessons Learned from the Faculty Mentoring Program, West Chester University, 2008–2011." *Mentoring & Tutoring: Partnership in Learning* 22 (2014) 56–73. https://doi.org/10.1080/13611267.2014.882606.

Beck, Frederick A. G., and Rosalind Thomas. "Greek Education." In *The Oxford Classical Dictionary*, edited by Simon Hornblower and Antony Spawforth, 487–89. 4th ed. Oxford: Oxford University Press, 2012.

Benedek, Mónika, and David Vinden. *Harmony Through Relative Solfa: A Practical Approach Using Fine Music Examples Selected from Different Eras*. 2nd ed. London: Kodály Centre, 2020.

Benedictines of Solesmes, ed. *The Liber Usualis*. Solesmes, Fr.: Descleé & Co., 1956.

Berkeley, Lennox. "Letters to Nadia Boulanger, 1929–74." In *Lennox Berkeley and Friends: Writings, Letters and Interviews*, edited by Peter Dickinson, 45–88. Woodbridge, UK: Boydell & Brewer, 2012.

Best, Harold M. "Music Curricula in the Future." *Arts Education Policy Review* 94 (1992) 2–7. https://doi.org/10.1080/10632913.1992.9936901.

Boethius, Anicius M. S. "Fundamentals of Music." In Strunk, *Source Readings in Music History*, 2:37–43.

Bomba, Andreas. Program notes for *Cantata BWV 182*. Bach Collegium Stuttgart and Gächinger Kantorei Stuttgart. Helmut Rilling. Vol. 55 of Kantaten/Cantates. Hänssler, 2000, compact disc.

Brooks, Jeanice. "Noble et grande servant de la musique: Telling the Story of Nadia Boulanger's Conducting Career." *Journal of Musicology* 14 (1996) 92–116.

Brown, Clive. *Classical & Romantic Performance Practice, 1750–1900*. Oxford: Oxford University Press, 2002.

Burnett, Charles. "Perceiving Sound in the Middle Ages." In *Hearing History: A Reader*, edited by Mark M. Smith, 69–84. London: University of Georgia Press, 2004.

Burns, Robert B. *Introduction to Research Methods*. 4th ed. London: SAGE, 2000.

Campbell, Don G. *Master Teacher: Nadia Boulanger*. Washington, DC: Pastoral, 1984.

Candy, Linda. *The Creative Reflective Practitioner: Research Through Making and Practice*. London: Routledge, 2019.

Carr, Marsha L., et al. "Learning to Lead: Higher Education Faculty Explore Self-Mentoring." *International Journal of Evidence-Based Coaching and Mentoring* 13 (2015) 1–13.

Castanheira, Patricia S. P. "Mentoring for Educators' Professional Learning and Development." *International Journal of Mentoring and Coaching in Education* 5 (2016) 334–46.

Chase, Robert. *Dies Irae: A Guide to Requiem Music*. Lanham, MD: Scarecrow, 2003.

Clutterbuck, David A., et al. Introduction to *The SAGE Handbook of Mentoring*, edited by David A. Clutterbuck et al., 1–10. London: SAGE, 2017. https://doi.org/10.4135/9781526402011.n1.

Cohen, Louis, et al. *Research Methods in Education*. 7th ed. Oxon, UK: Routledge, 2011.

Conlon, Joan C., ed. *Wisdom, Wit, and Will: Women Choral Conductors on Their Art*. Chicago: GIA, 2009.

Conomos, Dimitri. "Early Christian and Byzantine Music: History and Performance." Greek Orthodox Archdiocese of America, Nov. 15, 2012. http://www.asbm.goarch.org/articles/early-christian-and-byzantine-music-history-and-performance/.

Cox, Howard H., ed. *The Calov Bible of J. S. Bach*. Studies in Musicology 92. Ann Arbor: UMI Research Press, 1985.

Csikszentmihalyi, Mihaly. *Flow: The Psychology of Optimal Experience*. New York: Harper and Row, 1990.

Darling, Lu Ann W. "Self-Mentoring Strategies." *Journal of Nursing Administration* 15 (1985) 42–43. https://doi.org/10.1097/00005110-198504000-00010.

Davis, Dannielle Joy, et al. "Peer Mentoring and Inclusion in Writing Groups." In *The SAGE Handbook of Mentoring and Coaching in Education*, edited by Sarah J. Fletcher and Carol A. Mullen, 445–56. London: SAGE, 2012.

Dettwiler, Peggy. "Developing Aural Skills Through Vocal Warm-Ups: Historical Overview of Pedagogical Approaches and Applications for Choral Directors." *Choral Journal* 30 (1989) 13–15, 17–20. http://www.jstor.com/stable/23547783.

Dominguez, Nora, and Frances Kochan. "Defining Mentoring: An Elusive Search for Meaning and a Path for the Future." In *The Wiley International Handbook of Mentoring: Paradigms, Practices, Programs, and Possibilities*, edited by Beverly J. Irby et al., 3–18. Wiley Handbooks in Education. Hoboken, NJ: John Wiley & Sons, 2020.

Doukhan, Lilianne. *In Tune with God*. Hagerstown, MD: Autumn, 2010.

Elliott, David J. *Music Matters: A New Philosophy of Music Education*. New York: Oxford University Press, 1995.

———. *Praxial Music Education: Reflections and Dialogues*. Oxford: Oxford University Press, 2005.

Elliott, David J., and Marissa Silverman. *Music Matters: A Philosophy of Music Education*. 2nd ed. New York: Oxford University Press, 2015.

Emmons, Shirlee, and Constance Chase. *Prescriptions for Choral Excellence*. Chicago: GIA, 2006.

Fauré, Gabriel. *Requiem*. Edited and translated by John Rutter. 1893 ed. Oxford: Oxford University Press, 1984.

Feuchtwanger-Sarig, Naomi. "Chanting to the Hand: Some Preliminary Observations on the Origins of the Torah Pointer." *Studia Rosenthaliana* 37 (2004) 3–35. https://www.jstor.org/stable/41482486.

Forkel, Johann Nikolaus. *Johann Sebastian Bach: His Life, Art and Work*. Translated by Charles Sanford Terry. New York: Harcourt, Brace and Howe, 1920.

Fuller, David. "Notes Inégales." Grove Music Online, 2001. https://www.oxfordmusiconline.com/grovemusic/view/10.1093/gmo/9781561592630.001.0001/omo-9781561592630-e-0000020126.

Gaizauskas, Barbara R. "The Harmony of the Spheres." *Journal of the Royal Astronomical Society of Canada* 68 (1974) 146–51.

Galkin, Elliott. *The History of Orchestral Conducting: Theory and Practice*. New York: Pendragon, 1988.

Gardiner, John Eliot. *Bach: Music in the Castle of Heaven*. New York: Knopf, 2013.

Gardner, Howard. *Multiple Intelligences: New Horizons in Theory and Practice.* New York: Basic, 2006.

———. *Frames of Mind.* 2nd ed. New York: Basic, 2011.

Garvey, Bob, et al. "First-Person Mentoring." *Career Development International* 1 (1996) 10–14.

Geck, Martin. *Johann Sebastian Bach: Life and Work.* Translated by John Hargraves. Orlando: Harcourt, 2006.

Gerson-Kiwi, Edith. "Cheironomy." Grove Music Online, 2001. Revised by David Hiley. https://doi.org/10.1093/gmo/9781561592630.article.05510.

Glass, Philip. *Words Without Music.* London: Faber, 2015.

Gordon, Edwin. *Advanced Measures of Music Audiation.* Chicago: GIA, 1989.

Gordon Institute for Music Learning. "Audiation." GIML, n.d. https://giml.org/mlt/audiation/.

Green, Elizabeth A. H., and Mark Gibson. *The Modern Conductor.* 7th ed. Upper Saddle River, NJ: Pearson Prentice Hall, 2004.

Guido d'Arezzo. "Epistle Concerning an Unknown Chant." In Strunk, *Source Readings in Music History*, 2:214–18.

———. "Guidonian Hand." MS Canon. Liturg. 216. f.168 recto. Bodleian Libraries, University of Oxford.

———. "Prologue to His Antiphoner." In Strunk, *Source Readings in Music History*, 2:211–14.

———. "Ut Queant Laxis." In *Ezer Év Kórusa* [A thousand years of choral music], edited by Forrai Miklós, 14. Budapest: Musica, 1977.

Haines, John. "The Origins of the Musical Staff." *Musical Quarterly* 91 (2008) 327–78.

Hart, John T., Jr. "The Status of Music Education Conducting Curricula, Practices, and Values." *Journal of Music Teacher Education* 28 (2018) 1–15. https://doi.org/10.1177/1057083718783464.

Heller, Wendy. *Music in the Baroque: Western Music in Context.* Norton History. New York: Norton, 2014.

Holmes, William T., and Marsha Carr. "Motivating Language and Self-Mentoring: A Training Program Supporting the Development of Leaders in Organizations." *Development and Learning in Organizations* 31 (2017). 4–5. https://doi.org/10.1108/DLO-02-2017-0010.

Holst, Imogen. *Conducting a Choir.* Oxford: Oxford University Press, 1990.

Hornby, Emma. "On Guido's Handiwork." *Early Music* 30 (2002) 123–24.

Houlahan, Micheál, and Philip Tacka. *From Sound to Symbol: Fundamentals of Music.* 2nd ed. New York: Oxford University Press, 2012.

Hughes, Andrew, and Edith Gerson-Kiwi. "Solmization." Grove Music Online, 2001. https://doi.org/10.1093/gmo/9781561592630.article.26154.

Irby, Beverly J., et al. "Epistemological Beginnings of Mentoring." In *The Wiley International Handbook of Mentoring: Paradigms, Practices, Programs, and Possibilities*, edited by Beverly J. Irby et al., 19–28. Wiley Handbooks in Education. Hoboken, NJ: John Wiley & Sons, 2020.

Ittzés, Mihály. "Zoltán Kodály, 1882–1967: Honorary President of ISME, 1964–1967." *International Journal of Music Education* 22 (2004) 131–47. https://doi.org/10.1177/0255761404044015.

Jaccard, Jerry. *A Tear in the Curtain: The Musical Diplomacy of Erzšébet Szönyi.* New York: Lang, 2016.

Jerome, St. "Commentary on the Epistle of Paul to the Ephesians." In Strunk, *Source Readings in Music History*, 2:126–28.

John Chrysostom, St. "Exposition of Psalm 41." In Strunk, *Source Readings in Music History*, 2:123–26.

Jones, Ann Howard, et al. "Analyzing the Choral-Orchestral Score." In Conlon, *Wisdom, Wit, and Will*, 13–39.

Jones, D., et al. "Musicians as Researchers—Insight or Insanity?" In *International Society for Music Education: 32nd World Conference on Music Education*, edited by David Forrest and Louise Godwin, 147–57. Malvern, Aus.: International Society of Music Education, 2016.

Jordan, James. *Evoking Sound: Fundamentals of Choral Conducting.* 2nd ed. Chicago: GIA, 2009.

———. *Evoking Sound: The Choral Rehearsal.* 2 vols. Chicago: GIA, 2007, 2008.

Joseph, Miriam. *The Trivium: The Liberal Arts of Logic, Grammar, and Rhetoric.* Philadelphia: Dry, 2002.

Karpinski, Gary S. *Aural Skills Acquisition: The Development of Listening, Reading and Performing Skills in College-Level Musicians.* New York: Oxford University Press, 2000.

Kaulkin, Michael. "What Is Musicianship?" Medium, Dec. 5, 2009. https://medium.com/@michaelkaulkin/what-is-musicianship-49b40031476a.

Kerka, Sandra. "New Perspectives on Mentoring." ERIC Resource Center, 1998. ERIC Digest 194. https://files.eric.ed.gov/fulltext/ED418249.pdf.

King, Aleta. "Handing On the Baton: When Mentee Becomes Mentor." Paper presented at Second International Conducting Studies Conference, Oxford Conducting Institute, St Anne's College, University of Oxford, June 22, 2018.

———. "That's a Lot of Dots!" In *Australian Society for Music Education: XXI National Conference Proceedings*, edited by David Forrest and Louise Godwin, 45–51. Melbourne: ASME, 2017.

Kodály, Zoltán. "Who Is a Good Musician?" In *The Selected Writings of Zoltán Kodály*, edited by Ferenc Bónis, translated by Lili Halápy and Fred Macnicol, 185–200. London: Boosey & Hawkes, 1974.

Lancer, Natalie, et al. *Techniques for Coaching and Mentoring.* 2nd ed. Abingdon, UK: Routledge, 2016.

Leaver, Robin A., ed. *J. S. Bach and Scripture: Glosses from the Calov Bible Commentary.* St. Louis: Concordia, 1985.

Levitin, Daniel J. *This Is Your Brain on Music.* London: Atlantic, 2008.

Levitin, Daniel J., and Scott T. Grafton. "Measuring the Representational Space of Music with fMRI: A Case Study with Sting." *Neurocase* 22 (2016) 548–57. https://doi.org/10.1080/13554794.2016.1216572.

Luther, Martin. "Wittenberg Gesangbuch." In Strunk, *Source Readings in Music History*, 3:361–62.

McAdams, Stephen, and Emmanuel Bigand, eds. *Thinking in Sound: The Cognitive Psychology of Human Audition*. Oxford: Oxford University Press, 2001.

McCarthy, Marie, and J. Scott Goble. "Music Education, Philosophy of." Grove Music Online, 2011. https://doi.org/10.1093/gmo/9781561592630.article.A2093412.

McKinnon, James. "Boethius." In Strunk, *Source Readings in Music History*, 2:137.

———. "Guido of Arezzo." In Strunk, *Source Readings in Music History*, 2:211.

Monsaingeon, Bruno. *Nadia Boulanger: Mademoiselle*. EuroArts/Naxos, 1977. DVD.

Monsaingeon, Bruno, and Nadia Boulanger. *Mademoiselle: Conversations with Nadia Boulanger*. Translated by Robyn Marsack. Manchester, UK: Carcanet, 1985.

Moses, Don V., et al. *Face to Face with Orchestra and Chorus: A Handbook for Choral Conductors*. 2nd ed. Bloomington: Indiana University Press, 2004.

Nectoux, Jean-Michel. *Gabriel Fauré: A Musical Life*. Cambridge: Cambridge University Press, 1991.

———. *Gabriel Fauré: His Life Through His Letters*. London: Boyars, 1984.

Niceta of Remesiana. "On the Benefit of Psalmody." In Strunk, *Source Readings in Music History*, 2:128–31.

Noble, Western. *Achieving Choral Blend Through Standing Position*. Chicago: GIA, 2005. DVD.

Orledge, Robert. *Gabriel Fauré*. London: Eulenburg, 1979.

Parrot, Andrew. *The Essential Bach Choir*. Woodbridge, UK: Boydell, 2000.

Pesce, Dolores. "Guido d'Arezzo, Ut Queant Laxis, and Musical Understanding." In *Music Education in the Middle Ages and the Renaissance*, edited by Susan Forscher Weiss et al., 25–36. Bloomington: Indiana University Press, 2010.

———, ed. and trans. *Guido d'Arezzo's "Regule Rithmice," "Prologus in Antiphonarium," and "Epistola ad Michahelem": A Critical Text and Translation with an Introduction, Annotations, Indices, and New Manuscript Inventories*. Musicological Studies 73. Ottawa: Institute of Medieval Music, 1999.

Plato. *The Republic*. Translated by Desmond Lee. Penguin Classics. London: Penguin, 2007.

Potter, Caroline. *Nadia and Lili Boulanger*. London: Routledge, 2006. https://doi.org/10.4324/9781315597188.

Proust, Dominique. "Harmony of the Spheres: From Pythagoras to Voyager 2." *The Role of Astronomy in Society and Culture: Proceedings of the International Astronomical Union Symposium* 260 (2011) 358–67.

Rainbow, Bernarr. "French Time Names." Grove Music Online, 2001. https://doi.org/10.1093/gmo/9781561592630.article.10213.

Rainbow, Bernarr, and Charles Edward McGuire. "Tonic Sol-Fa." Grove Music Online, 2001. https://doi.org/10.1093/gmo/9781561592630.article.28124.

Reid, Anna, et al. "From Expert Student to Novice Professional: Higher Education and Sense of Self in the Creative and Performing Arts." *Music Education Research* 21 (2019) 399–413. https://doi.org/10.1080/14613808.2019.1632279.

Reimer, Bennett. *A Philosophy of Music Education.* 2nd ed. Englewood Cliffs, NJ: Prentice Hall, 1989.

———. *A Philosophy of Music Education: Advancing the Vision.* 3rd ed. Englewood Cliffs, NJ: Prentice Hall, 2003.

Robinson, Ken. *The Element: How Finding Your Passion Changes Everything.* New York: Penguin, 2009.

Rorem, Ned. Review of *Nadia Boulanger: A Life in Music*, by Léonie Rosenstiel. *New York Times*, May 23, 1982. https://www.nytimes.com/1982/05/23/books/the-composer-and-the-music-teacher.html.

Seaman, Christopher. *Inside Conducting.* Rochester: University of Rochester Press, 2013.

Serafine, Mary L. *Music as Cognition: The Development of Thought in Sound.* New York: Columbia University Press, 1988.

Schering, Arnold. *Johann Sebastian Bachs Leipziger Kirchenmusik.* Leipzig: Breitkopf & Ha̎rtel, 1936.

Schön, Donald A. *Educating the Reflective Practitioner: Toward a New Design for Teaching and Learning in the Professions.* Higher Education. New York: Jossey-Bass, 1987.

Schumann, Robert. *Advice to Young Musicians.* Gutenberg, Feb. 28, 2009. Translated by Henry Hugo Pierson. EBook 28219. https://www.gutenberg.org/files/28219/28219-h/28219-h.htm.

Schweitzer, Albert. *J. S. Bach.* Translated by Ernest Newman. 2 vols. New York: Dover, 1966.

Simons, Harriet. "Nadia and Me." In Conlon, *Wisdom, Wit, and Will*, 323–30.

Southerland, William. "Giving Music a Hand: Conducting History in Practice and Pedagogy." *Choral Journal* 59 (2019) 30–43. https://www-jstor-org.ezproxy.library.sydney.edu.au/stable/26601977.

Spitta, Philipp. *Johann Sebastian Bach: His Work and Influence on the Music of Germany, 1685–1750.* Translated by Clara Bell and J. A. Fuller-Maitland. 3 vols. London: Novello, Ewer & Co., 1885.

Spitzer, John, et al. "Conducting." Grove Music Online, 2001. https://doi.org/10.1093/gmo/9781561592630.article.06266.

Stahl, Christina M., and Michael Stegemann. Preface to *Messe de Requiem*, op. 48, by Gabriel Fauré, vii–x. Translated by Steve Taylor. 1900 ed. Kassel: Bärenereiter, 2011.

Strunk, Oliver, ed. *Source Readings in Music History.* Revised by Leo Treitler. Rev. ed. 7 vols. New York: Norton, 1998.

Szabó, Helga. *The Kodály Concept of Music Education.* Edited and translated by Geoffry Russell-Smith. London: Boosey & Hawkes, 1969.

Tavierne, Kim M. "Conducting: How It Came to Be." Presentation at Research and Scholarship Symposium 21, Cedarville University, Cedarville, OH, Apr. 1, 2015.

Thackar, Markand. *On the Principles and Practice of Conducting*. Rochester: University of Rochester Press, 2016.

Tomlinson, Gary. Introduction to sect. 3, "The Renaissance." In Strunk, *Source Readings in Music History*, 3:281–88.

Varga, Bálint András. "Nadia Boulanger." In *From Boulanger to Stockhausen: Interviews and a Memoir*, 187–96. Eastman Studies in Music. Woodbridge, UK: Boydell & Brewer, 2013.

Vujović, Ida. "Between Building Foundational Skills and Instilling Self-Guided Learning: Solfège Pedagogy in Higher Music Education." Research Catalogue, 2014. https://doi.org/10.22501/koncon.87162.

Vujović, Ida, and Banka Bogunović. "Metacognitive Strategies in Learning Sight-Singing." *Psihološka Istraživanja* 15 (2012) 115–33.

Williams, Peter. *Bach: A Musical Biography*. Cambridge: Cambridge University Press, 2016.

SELECTED AUDIO RECORDINGS

Bach, J. S. *Bach Cantatas*. Monteverdi Choir, English Baroque Soloists. John Eliot Gardiner. Vol. 21. Soli Deo Gloria, 2000, compact disc.

———. *Cantata BWV 182*. Bach Collegium Stuttgart and Gächinger Kantorei Stuttgart. Helmut Rilling. Tracks 1–8. Vol. 55 of Kantaten/Cantates. Hänssler, 2000, compact disc.

———. *Cantata BWV 182*. Sydney Conservatorium Chamber Choir and Baroque Orchestra. Neil McEwan. 2004, MP3. In the author's possession.

———. *Complete Cantatas*. Amsterdam Baroque Orchestra and Choir. Ton Koopman. Vol. 2. Challenge, 1995, compact disc.

———. *Das Kantatenwerk*. Concentus Musicus Wien. Nikolaus Harnoncourt. Vol. 42. Teldec, 1988, compact disc.

Fauré, Gabriel. *Requiem*. Cambridge Singers and City of London Sinfonia. John Rutter. Conifer, 1984, compact disc.

———. *Requiem*. Chapelle Royale and Ensemble Musique Oblique. Philippe Herreweghe. Harmonia Mundi, 1988, compact disc.

———. *Requiem*. BBC Symphony Orchestra and Chorus. Nadia Boulanger. EMI, 1948, compact disc.